**Sports**
**Illustrated**
**Cruise Books**

# INSIDE PASSAGE TO ALASKA

## A SPORTS ILLUSTRATED CRUISE BOOK

*By Morten Lund*

*With photographs by Clyde Banks*
*and by the author*

J. B. LIPPINCOTT COMPANY • PHILADELPHIA *&* NEW YORK

MAP DRAWN BY ALLEN BEECHEL

This book is dedicated to Portrey
and to Banks, who got us through;
and to my parents, who taught me
to enjoy the water

# Contents

JUNEAU ★

TAKU RIVER

TAKU HARBOR

ALASKA

ALEXANDER
ARCHIPELAGO

STEPHENS PASSAGE

FORDS TERROR

LE CONTE GLACIER

PETERSBURG

CLARENCE STRAIT

BELL ISLAND

BEHM CANAL

WALKER COVE

KETCHIKAN

ALASKA

CANADA

DIXON ENTRANCE

PRINCE RUPERT

BRITISH COLUMBIA

LOWE INLET

PACIFIC OCEAN

QUEEN CHARLOTTE ISLANDS

BUTEDALE

MILBANKE
SOUND

BELLA BELLA

RIVERS
INLET

CALVERT ISLAND

DUNCANBY LANDING

QUEEN
CHARLOTTE
SOUND

PHILLIPS ARM

STUART ISLAND

PRINCESS
LOUISA
INLET

ALERT BAY

JOHNSTONE

CAMPBELL
RIVER

STRAIT

PENDER HARBOR

VANCOUVER ISLAND

STRAIT OF GEORGIA

VANCOUVER

BIG SUCIA

BELLINGHAM

NANAIMO

CANADA

U.S.A.

VICTORIA

SAN
JUAN
ISLANDS

PORT
ANGELES

MAIN ROUTE

SIDE TRIPS

HURRICANE
RIDGE

OLYMPIC PENINSULA

SEATTLE ★

PUGET SOUND

WASHINGTON

# 1

## *The Birth of the Cruise: Seattle*

**T**HIS is the story of a carefully planned cruise into Alaska, conceived at *Sports Illustrated*. It is a reasonable sort of cruise, but, within that limitation, the largest and most adventuresome undertaking that could have been devised to fill a four-week voyage.

The cruise was made along the Inside Passage. This is the course that yachtsmen follow through the high rock islands and shores winding north out of the United States into British Columbia and Alaska—sometimes protected, sometimes open to the Pacific, a course running a thousand miles from Seattle to Juneau and beyond.

The Inside Passage, as I found it, was magnificent: a stretch of mountain-hemmed sea, a sea corridor walled with peaks. The passage runs along a drowned coast: a sunken range massive as the Rockies and capped with snow, burdened with monstrous glaciers and cleaved with great rivers roaring out to sea.

It is an exhilarating shore. The sheer, thrusting Coast Mountains run down under the sea as well as above it. You cruise under thousand-foot cliffs that come billowing straight out of ocean, rising six, seven, eight thousand feet above the cabin of the yacht; you run in maelstrom and counter-maelstrom pouring through narrow waists of passages 50, 60, or 70 miles inland; you move quietly after salmon in the hush of an evening; your cruiser sits in a tidal pool where the breeze presses down from cool snow fields above and the snow melt rushes over the rocks to the sea.

It is a progression away from civilization. North of Vancouver Island, room service is out—until Juneau. The prehistoric forest sweeps from the heights straight down to the sea, 200-foot cascades plunge into the tides, seals sun them-

9

The Norseman outboard cruiser, stern to, with twin Mercury engines pushing.

selves on the quiet surfaces of the inner ice floe, and the 50-foot, ugly black back of the whale lies awash; the ice pack surges and grinds in the glacial arms, and icebergs come crashing down into the chilled waters; bears roam the beaches, and salmon drive restlessly up the rivers; the stiff 5-foot club dorsal of the killer whale breaks the surface in the solitudes of seldom-seen fjords. Here is one of the last great adventure coasts left to us.

This cruise was designed to provide a model for yachtsmen who might be inspired to duplicate the voyage. The bare bones of the cruise plan can be seen in the map on page 8. The main course of the cruise runs straight for Juneau, with such deviations as common sense and customs regulations dictate. (The smaller maps divide this course into three sections.) Off the main course are some fifteen side trips, chosen from a hundred possibilities that interested us. These are the high points. Each side trip adds an experience that previous parts of the cruise have not provided.

The fine boating country along the Inside Passage was, fortunately, left untouched by the 1964 earthquake in Alaska. The reportage on the quake gave the erroneous impression that most of Alaska had dropped into the Pacific. Actually, the damage was confined largely to Anchorage and a few outlying islands. Even in Anchorage the damage was localized. Most of the outlying parts of the town were shaken but intact after the quake. Within a month, every single Anchorage motel and hotel was open for tourist business as usual. As for the Inside Passage, what was true of the beautiful waterway before the quake is true afterwards: all charts for the southern part of the coast read exactly the way they always have, and this southern coast is where the *Sports Illustrated* cruise takes place.

The Inside Passage runs right out of Puget Sound. A voyage up the Passage can start anywhere in the Sound, but there are good reasons, if you come overland or up the coast, to start in Seattle. For one thing, it has the finest tuning-up facilities in the Northwest. For another, a stay in the city is a delight.

Our cruise, therefore, started in Seattle. A crack *Sports Illustrated* correspondent, Dolly Connelly, of Bellingham, Washington, had persuaded two of the best cruising men in the Northwest to obtain a hull, ready it, and guide the cruise north from Seattle. Those two were Philip Portrey and Clyde Banks, both of Bellingham.

I preceded Portrey and Banks to Seattle, partly because I wanted to look around the city. The houses of Seattle lie sprinkled like spilled salt from the cliffs of Puget Sound to the marinas and docks that finger out into Lake Union and Lake Washington: it is a city surrounded by water and one whose boat-mindedness makes its services to yachtsmen unexcelled.

You can take the measure of the town's dedication to boats by going over to Norman Ledger's Marine Charters on Lake Union. Ledger's rental operation carries everything from fishing dories to 50-foot inboards. (Given notice, Ledger can arrange a charter all the way to Alaska.)

Lake Union is a sort of industrial way station between Puget Sound and Lake Washington, the latter being a 26-mile-long water extravaganza that bounds Seattle to the east. Lake Washington draws an incredible flotilla of boats out to play on almost any day of the week. One is enveloped in a swarm of outboards, inboards, sloops, fishing rigs, cruising rigs, racing rigs, and rowboats—all beating about the lake like happy, erratic water bugs.

The skilled mechanics and engineers at Boeing and at the machine shops around town like to go screaming down the lake with a pair of motors singing synchronously. Nobody seems to buy anything less than a 35-horse engine. Motorboat men stop each other in the middle of the lake and talk rpm's, drives, and prop angles. Down at the south end of the lake, by the first floating bridge, is the Gold Cup hydroplane course where, three years out of four, Seattleites expect one of their drivers to defend or win the Gold Cup, the country's number-one racing motorboat trophy.

The repair and fitting-out establishment that keeps this huge pleasure fleet on the water fills more than sixty marinas on the lakes and on Puget Sound. For outboarders, there are marinas like Bryant's (Evinrude) and Pacific Fish and Trading (Mercury). An outboard marina can rig, launch, and tune a boat in a single day. Inboarders can pick from a half-dozen outstanding places, the best known being Ledger's.

Having, as I did, a layover while your boat is being readied, allows enough time for sampling the city. Sea-food restaurants are good—you can have a memorable lunch at Ivar's Fifth Avenue on oysters alone. There is a small, plain Miyako that serves sea food Japanese-style: octopus slices, rice soup, raw fish, and tea. The Space Needle restaurant still revolves pleasantly, and bone-dry martinis enhance the motion. Above Lake Union, Canlis' famous restaurant offers a marine view and the best steak west of Chicago and east of Honolulu (there's a Canlis'

*12*

there, too). In the late hours there are sophisticated night clubs like the Colony, where Norm Bobrors discovered Pat Suzuki. There is a deliciously potent rum punch to be had at the Outrigger Restaurant.

The morning after I had tried my endurance at the Outrigger, the rest of my crew came into town. They had brought the boat, a 24-foot Norseman outboard hull, from Bellingham. She had just come off the builder's ways.

Phil Portrey, somewhat over thirty, had spent half his life on the Inside Passage waters. He was of medium height, wiry, and highly charged. Clyde Banks, the official expedition photographer and a friend of Portrey's, was somewhat younger, tall, blond, and strongly put together. Both looked as if they had the constitution needed for the long run. I was older than Banks, younger than Portrey—and softer than either.

We had our agreements and disagreements on equipment, but this was Portrey's territory and he knew what he wanted. We went out almost immediately to Pacific Fish and Trading, where the boat was having windshield wipers installed and was being given a final tune-up by the Mercury Outboard experts who were supplying the twin 60-hp engines that were going to push us to Alaska.

There are two ways to use engine power when you travel to Alaska: you can take the Inside Passage in fast, long spurts or in short, slow hops. The former is a magnificent way to cover the distance and sometimes an extremely uncomfortable one. The slow-and-easy way calls for more stops, more planning, and probably two summer vacations spent traveling the Inside Passage, rather than one. Portrey, Banks and I were going to do it in fast-and-furious style. We had contracted to cover the distance from Seattle to Juneau and back within four weeks, including, on our way north, well over a dozen side trips varying from a day's length to a few hours. We had to be able to run fast and far; we had to be able to run from weather; we wanted to be able to bite off 100 miles in the morning, leaving the afternoons free for our fishing and exploring. All of this we could do with our twin Mercurys. Our power would give us a top speed of 35 mph and a cruising speed somewhat over 30. The hull was a full cabin, high freeboard design, built of $\frac{3}{8}$-inch marine plywood. It had 5-foot headroom, three bunks, and a big cockpit that could be half covered in a minute by unfolding the convertible canvas top that lay on the windshield frame. (In the concluding pages, I discuss more fully the matter of power and philosophy, particularly in relation to hull types.)

Twenty-four feet is a good three-man hull size for extended outboard cruising.

In a 20-foot boat we would have been crowded. In a 30-foot outboard, we would have had more boat than we needed, and we would have had to carry correspondingly more power to get our 35-mph top speed.

The Norseman's topsides were painted a bright yellow, per Banks's orders. He said that nothing showed up so well in color slides as that particular yellow, and it would show up easily against the darker sea if the Coast Guard should be out looking for us. He added that he did not expect the occasion to arise.

As we went over the charts, we mentally divided the Inside Passage into three main sections:

The first section, off the state of Washington and lower British Columbia, runs through the 172 islands of the San Juans on the United States–Canada border. The first section course is protected by the 300-mile-long bulk of Vancouver Island. This protection makes the initial leg an ideal preparation for the huskier kind of cruising in the next two sections.

The second section, off upper British Columbia, is reached by crossing Queen Charlotte Sound, a 65-mile stretch open to the Pacific. The protection along this section is thinner, but adequate. The shoreline increases in beauty and the salmon in size.

The last section, off Alaska, is attained by crossing Dixon Entrance, another large open stretch. Once over Dixon, the cruising goes into wilder and less friendly water, but the rewards—glacier fields, ice floes, pods of whale—are correspondingly great.

Having plotted our cruise in the rough, we turned in and slept our first night aboard the Norseman hull, ready for an early start. The outlook was for a four-week cruise that would go well over 2,000 miles, and have a good deal of adventure in store. On our first day we would head for the San Juan Islands, the natural first landfall on an Inside Passage cruise. We would find our first pleasure in an easy anchorage at Fossil Cove on Big Sucia, in the San Juans.

# 2

## *Islands in the Sun*

AT SEVEN O'CLOCK on a bright clean July morning, we had our first meal on board. The Norseman bobbed quietly at its float beside the pier. We had spent the night thrashing around in our unaccustomed bunks. Mine was just short of my height—something like the medieval torture cage in which a man could neither quite stand up nor quite lie down.

After breakfast, Portrey stood at the helm; Banks and I gathered in the lines; the two Mercs turned over with a beautifully competent roar. We backed off the float. Then the engines quit, and a brisk little local current seemed to be heading us right for a brace of pilings under the pier. The starter wouldn't start the engines. Portrey threw the engines into reverse, figuring that whatever was wrong with the forward-throttle connections, the reverse connections might be working. The engines started in reverse, Portrey shifted and gunned forward, skinned by the pilings, and took off. This incident proved to be a portent, not for the engines, which performed almost flawlessly thereafter, but for Portrey, who could be relied upon to make the right move when it counted.

The Norseman skipped across Lake Union toward Ballard Locks. The upper gate opened for us; the lower gate freed us and we went shooting out into the salt.

Puget Sound was gorgeous: the houses of Seattle gave back the morning light, the sky was blue and the sea (to my eye) looked fairly smooth. I went below to work over some notes. Above, Portrey revved the engines to full cruising throttle and nosed the Norseman into the bright, sparkling chop. The effect below was like being trapped in a snare drum that was rolling down a flight of stairs. I quickly got back into the cockpit, where the heavy things like gas tanks and motors are located, and also the center of pitch on an outboard. It was a lot more bearable here, but for a while I felt as if I was sharing a bunk with a pneumatic hammer. There was no cause for alarm: the sensation became normal as the trip progressed. I did, however, give up any idea of working below while Portrey was trying to make time.

We were on our 100-mile run to the San Juans, via Deception Pass. I had the twin throttles under hand for a while: we took turn and turn about at the helm to keep fresh. It took me some time before the act of scanning the surface became automatic, and at 30 mph it had better be automatic. I found that the throttles had to be pushed up a bit once in a while, but there was little else to worry about except driftwood and the wake of another boat: a light inland lake rig can bounce over an oncoming wake, but the somewhat heftier cruising rig must slow down or else the crew and the hull are thrown against each other with considerable force. The Norseman handled like a sports car. She leaned into turns beautifully and came around like a cat chasing its tail. In moderately strong waves she ran true and dry.

We already had begun to balance off against each other, the essential process of becoming a crew. Clyde Banks was an easy-going, good-humored, never-tiring workhorse. His instinct for photography never seemed to becloud his sense of what had to be done in the way of work. I was a perfect counterpart: worried, ill-humored, looking up at each noise. I hadn't quite got used to the idea that $\frac{3}{8}$-inch plywood was sufficient protection between us and all that lay in the sea.

Once on an outboard, Phil Portrey—a well-to-do service station manager in daily life—became a happy pirate. As one of the original outboard bugs in the area years before when the standard top power was in the 20-hp range, Portrey had had a hopped-up 33-horse engine and, according to Banks, was known as "the terror of Puget." The only big thing that he ever ran into, though, was a whale.

"I was running for Seattle one evening," Portrey recalled, "coming from the San Juans, when all of a sudden the boat rose up, soft like, and the next thing I knew, I was headed back to the San Juans."

To starboard, as we talked, was Whidbey, a long, narrow island of fir and cedar, summer homes, and farms. We ran under the bridge at Deception Pass, the first navigation obstacle of any note. The Pacific was running in 10-knot whirls. Portrey fired the Norseman through without a pause, however.

In the San Juans: Portray pauses over chart book to find out what island is where.

Around the next island on our course we ran across a purse seiner, a 52-footer. Its seine was then rapidly closing on a school of salmon. Portrey idled the Norseman so that we could watch. The seiner had put out a little purse-seine skiff which carried one end of the huge net in a wide semicircle, enclosing the salmon. As we watched, the deck winches clattered on; now the circle began to tighten while one crewman, the "plunger," splashed methodically with a long cup-ended pole to create a wall of bubbles, intended to keep the salmon inside the purse lines. The primitive stratagem seemed to work, for, as slowly, inexorably, the whole seine was tightened, the hundreds of slithering, desperate bodies in the net became a silver burden which the net boom held at the surface of the water as the crew furiously piled the excess net on deck. A huge basket, the "brail," dipped into the writhing mass and dropped the salmon into the hold. The purse seiner had pulled its set.

Portrey made one other stop. He located some reef netters on Legoe Bay off Lummi Island for us. The reef net operation looked like a poor relation to purse-seining: a series of narrow double-enders linked by a submerged reef net in the path of salmon bound for Fraser River. We tied up to a double-ender and got on to watch. Each double-ender had its own ladder with a spotter perched on it. When the spotter saw a few salmon in the depths between two double-enders, the weighted net was winched up in a hurry. While we were there the average catch was something like three salmon. It was a relatively hopeless-looking method, but there are, I was told, times when the tide and the salmon run right and the pay-off is big.

As we were reluctantly leaving the Lummi shore line, Portrey explained that the purse seiners and reef netters were catching sockeye, the big commercial salmon in the Pacific. The sockeye run from 5 to 7 pounds, and bring about two dollars each wholesale. They are relatively small but powerful salmon. Those who have seen them run in the spawning rivers say that the strength they show is almost unbelievable.

The big sockeye runs are up the Fraser River to its tributaries, north of Seattle. The salmon we had seen were undoubtedly headed for there. The sockeye draw toward the Fraser after three years at sea, impelled by some biological clock. They circle off the river delta while the seiners and the rest take their toll. Then the rains come and the river freshens; the surge of increased current triggers the run; the fish head for the Fraser pasturage, beginning a metamorphosis from fish to breeding machine. Their stomachs close, they eat nothing; they draw up the river, slowly turning from a silver to a crimson, the flesh slowly softening, mottling black in the bruising battle through rapids and falls.

When they reach the spawning grounds, the female makes the redd; she fans deep holes for her eggs while roundabout the crimson, dying males go after each other, ripping and tearing, racing to hold their spot in the redd and to fertilize the eggs and die, drifting slowly down for the second and last time.

In the Lummi Islands: the purse seiner with her net floated and ready to haul.

The romantic aspect of the salmon is not important to the fisherman, but the existence of the salmon is. It gives the Inside Passage settlements their character, the inhabitants their livelihood, and the conversation its topic.

By the time we had gotten well away from the reef netters, it was late morning. We aimed the Norseman at the San Juans, intending to lunch there. By noon we could see the dark forested islands, floating on the bright haze under a high sun. We slid the Norseman into Fossil Cove on Big Sucia. Within the cove was a pleasant diversity typical of the islands. A group of public-spirited boatmen, first raising money to buy it, had deeded Sucia to the state. The state had built a wharf and cleared land ashore for cookouts and camping.

We lowered the dinghy and rowed ashore. Portrey led us into the forest a bit and there hanging begging was a lush crop of blackberries. We picked enthusiastically and then came back to the beach, where we stabbed about with shovels until we had a half-dozen clams apiece. Perhaps it was hunger that made the clams and berries so delicious; perhaps it was the pleasure of actually living, to some degree, off the land and the sea.

Fossil Cove is named for the dry, crumbling rock outcropping on one side of the harbor that contains authentic fossil material. We had a go at finding a fossil: we crumbled one flaky handful of rock after another to see if a fossil lay within. At the tenth handful, Portrey found one: a perfect little stone sea shell, a delicate design, some millions of years away from its life.

The San Juans are dangerous islands for yachtsmen dedicated to a 2,000-mile adventure cruise. The danger does not lie in the waters but in the magic attraction that the islands exercise. Sitting at Fossil Cove, one tends to ask, "Why go on when there is so much right here?" We resisted the lure, but before we left the archipelago we made a point of going around to nearby islands to demonstrate the variety available. (The islands we visited are too clustered to be shown individually on the maps in this book, but can be seen on any large map of the San Juans.)

We cruised toward Waldron, five miles to the west; it has some of the best salmon water in the United States. We fished, following the recipe of local fishermen: 60 feet of Monel line, 6-ounce sinker, a spoon baited with a bit of herring cut diagonally to make the spoon spin. Fishing being what it is, we had no luck in the short time that we had given ourselves to try.

Late in the afternoon, we went off to Friday Harbor on San Juan Island. The harbor is picturesque and Banks got off several rolls of Kodachrome. Portrey went to the Coast Guard station to place our itinerary on record. This formality is not required but it puts a description of the boat into the hands of the people who could help if we became overdue.

Banks told me that there is an oddity of sport on San Juan. The island has a

Banks conning the Norseman early in the trip. The land is Whidbey Island.

large Flemish rabbit population—so large that rabbit shooting is too easy to be sport. Netting is the thing. A local group of avid rabbit-netters go out in jalopies, armed with flashlights and net, to bag the bunnies. Our tight itinerary left us no time for netting, but yachtsmen who want to try this can get in touch with Ray Franklin at the Island Sky Ferries office; he can put you in contact with a hunt. (Franklin is a good source of information on any phase of cruising or camping in the San Juans. He is also delighted to lay on an aerial tour of the archipelago for anyone interested.)

We visited the other side of the island, stopping at Roche Harbor, a yacht haven with swimming pool, tennis, riding, and a historic hotel thoughtfully restored. The elegant marina welcomed us even though we did nothing more than take on water at the dock.

Preferring a primitive anchorage, we headed for Prevost Harbor on Stuart Island, 15 miles southwest of Sucia. The Norseman purred through the narrow channel and emerged in the regular millpond of a harbor. We dropped anchor and had a steak dinner, preceded by clams and finished off by blackberries.

Twilight moved in, ending the first day of our cruise. The moon came out full:

a world of dark water, forest, and glistening rock came alive in the soft summer night. We were in no hurry to leave. Our little tour was by no means an exhaustive catalog of the 172 islands. One could spend one's entire vacation here, easily. But if you want to go to Alaska and back in a summer, you'll have to limit yourself as we did . . . regretfully.

# 3

## Snow, Flowers, Crags, and Crabs

SKIING was a long way from my mind when I woke up the next morning in the middle of Prevost Harbor, but Portrey wanted to have the Norseman given a final check at her builder's yard in Bellingham, 40 miles due east on the mainland. I reminded him that we could engage a rental car in Bellingham, drive up to Heather Meadows on Mt. Baker in an hour and a half, rent skis, and have some of the finest summer skiing in the world 5,000 feet above sea level. But, our cruise complement being made up of one skier (me) and two nonskiers, we stayed in Bellingham only long enough to get our hull looked over.

Skippers who like to avoid cities the size of Seattle often begin their Inside Passage cruise at Bellingham. Besides being handier to get around in, it is 90 miles nearer Juneau. Bellingham's mechanics are plentiful and good. (If you go to Nanaimo or Victoria on the Canadian shore for repair, you may have to count on an Old World concept of time.) In Bellingham, Dick Crisp's Squalicum Fill Marina, which had previously installed the Mercury engines in our Norseman, lived up to a deserved reputation for excellence and speed.

Bellingham also is Portrey's and Banks's home town. Portrey knows the Inside Passage well. He's always glad to talk to boatmen. If you are in need of guidance on some special aspect of Alaska cruising, either he or Banks is the source to get in touch with.

We had a brief family scene with the Portreys and the Bankses and then took off for the San Juans, arriving in the island group about noon. At this point in the cruise, we could, following the *Sports Illustrated* itinerary, go north to Nanaimo to start the main part of the Inside Passage, or we could make a side trip to

Victoria 50 miles from Sucia, at the very bottom of Vancouver Island. We chose the latter.

## SIDE TRIP TO VICTORIA

The call of Victoria is strong for all tourists, but there is a hefty subconsideration in the quality of the food. It is a city for gourmets. It also is a city for those who love flowers, and for those who wish to see a remaining bastion of British colonial temper and art.

We came barreling into the harbor at Victoria, having first made certain that the intervening Strait of Juan de Fuca was relatively friendly. (If it had not been friendly, we could have motored to San Juan Island, taken a ferry to Sidney at the southeast corner of Vancouver Island and taxied to Victoria.)

As we approached the city we first became conscious of the two huge stone piles that dominate the Victoria waterfront. The smaller of these is the provincial Parliament building; the larger and grander, the Empress Hotel. One gets the feeling immediately that the town *could* get along without Parliament, if it came to a choice. Our first stop was at customs, as indeed it should be. There is still smuggling on the coast and any deviation from rules is regarded with suspicion. Customs is not complicated. The ship's captain identifies himself by means of a driver's license or other positive papers. He lists his passengers, and he lists the serial numbers on cameras and guns. (Unless he has previously obtained a Canadian hunting permit from the Canadian Game Commission, his rifles will be sealed at this point. No pistols are allowed in Canada.) That's all there is to it.

After this, we went to the Empress Hotel by cab. Victoria is all that a colonial capital ought to be: neat, clean, very Empire, lots of flowers and correct wear in the streets—except for the tourists, of course.

The Empress is no less impressive. It has long, long lawns and walls blanketed with ivy of a heroic thickness. The bellboys who took our little luggage were not bellboys at all, but ancient, faithful retainers. We got to our rooms to find that the beds stood a good 3 feet off the floor on old-fashioned legs. The bathtub of Victorian days had obviously struggled against being removed in favor of a glass-doored shower, but this unpleasantness was balanced by the fact that the telephone service was distinctly Victorian.

Downstairs again, we passed through *salles* as large as the waiting room at Grand Central Station. We had hoped to dine in one of them but found that

On Vancouver Island: Butchart's Gardens, north of Victoria.

service had stopped at 8 P.M. The maître d' suggested we try the *Princess Mary*, a coast steamer that had been hauled ashore to serve as a restaurant, with all its original nautical décor intact. The *Princess Mary* is reputed to have the best sea-food kitchen between Baja California and the Aleutians. The cabdriver was ecstatic over the place as he maneuvered us out to the section where the ex-ship lay. *Princess Mary* lived up to her notices. I had curried prawn, fresh salmon, deep fried oysters, blueberries, and coffee. It was a splendid performance. My portion of the bill (with wine) was five dollars American. Stuffed, happy, the crew went to bed within the great walls of the Empress.

The third day of the cruise dawned bright and clear. *Princess Mary's* cuisine plus a tour of the city might be enough of Victoria for most yachtsmen—it certainly was for Portrey and Banks—but not for me. They told me they'd stay put while I made further explorations. I had decided to take the flower-watcher's route: out Marine Drive and north 15 miles to an establishment known as Butchart's Gardens, a flower-lover's nirvana. After breakfast under worked oak beams amid acres of gleaming crystal in the Empress's breakfast nook, I phoned for a car and started up Marine Drive. This roadway is truly a many-splendored thing; it is a parade of homes and flowers, flowers and homes; some of the latter obviously sheltering bright geniuses of the garden art. There were wild impressionistic arrangements on the lawns: patterns of color, shape, and texture, hocks and ivy flung with calculated abandon over wall and lawn, pale yellow hedges set in purple bush, bronze-leafed trees, blood-red creepers running through perfect green grass, white bowers arching over doorways. What, I wondered, could Butchart's do to surpass this?

Butchart's is a stroke of philanthropy by a man who dug a big hole in the countryside to quarry granite and then decided to prove himself a fine fellow by having the landscape made presentable again. I parked in the vicinity of a small restaurant and was directed to climb a rise to the edge of the former quarry. I found myself standing before a realm of fantasy, a re-creation of the flowering folds of Eden. The trees and bushes and plants below me set each other off in a way that showed a sensitive mind had worked here, expressing a delight in color and a preference for order. The complement of form and hue was calculated to arouse emotions, and there was nothing old and stuffy about the emotions. I walked down the stone steps into the quarry and spent a good hour there.

Butchart's has other gardens as well. I went on to the small, brilliant rose garden, to the miniature formal Italian garden, and to a fine Japanese garden where plant and pond lie pleasantly mingled. I finally came out of the world of petals and made my way to the restaurant, tiny and very English, that rested at the center of this profusion. I ordered raspberries (fresh), cake, ice cream with tea, and, by all that's British, crumpets.

Once you have experienced Butchart's, your desire for tourism may wax, and there is another marvel that lies across the Strait of Juan de Fuca, a marvel even more spectacular. It is the highway to the interior of the Olympic Peninsula. The highway, playfully called "Heart O' the Hills Highway," stretches from Port Angeles (an hour's ferry ride from Victoria) into heights where the summer snow still lies. The trip is an exercise in pure sight-seeing. There are possibly only one or two other highways that afford comparable vistas.

Banks and Portrey, after a day of rest, were willing to go along on the Olympic Peninsula tour. At 9 A.M. on our fourth day out of Seattle we drove our rented car aboard a regular ocean liner of a ferry with a parking lot full of cars on the lower deck. From the upper deck, we watched the big ship move comfortably across the whitecaps now combing the Strait of Juan de Fuca, whitecaps which would have made a crossing in the Norseman rough work.

July on the Olympic Peninsula: snow blocks the Obstruction Point logging road.

27

### SIDE TRIP TO HURRICANE RIDGE

You enter the high Olympics via the technical triumph of 25 miles of blacktop thrust into the middle of the range. The road climbs into the tall timber. The trees get taller and straighter and soon they shear upward, 70 feet above the road, soaring trunks set close as grass. The ridges opposite the road, across the valley, take on a dark arrowhead pattern from the regular shape of the perfect tops, and the ridges cascade far down out of sight to the valley floors.

Just when it seems that the scenery can get no better, the road curves off into the blue and the car comes into sight of the entire Olympic range, pile after pile of dark green relieved by the lighter green of mountain meadows and, beyond

Snow and summer meet near Hurricane Ridge.

and above, the snow-peak lines, white and cool, edging back into the peninsula.

A few minutes more and you are at the end. Hurricane Ridge appears: slanting from it, a large mountain meadow, half flowered, half snowed under. On the ridge is a building and a parking lot. Once out of the car you see snow everywhere: in the moss, among the flowers, between the trees and on the peaks.

There is a chance to see the country more intimately by taking your car down a rough but passable road called the Obstruction Point logging road. This road goes on and on into the mountains, past blue lupine nodding next to swatches of snow on the glistening deep green sides of hills, past ridges whose shaded sides plunge into the afternoon dark below.

Black-tailed deer run about here like a pack of royal stag. On our way back,

The serried peaks of the Olympic range.

we almost ran down six of them; they were stationed in various calendar poses across the road—a flock of big-eared jaywalkers. We came to a stop. *We* had to wait for *them*; they made no move except to switch their tails impatiently when we leaned on the horn and shouted for room to pass. In their own good time, they moved off and we circled down to the darkening plain.

I had one further desire before leaving the peninsula. I wanted to detour to Dungeness, and sit down to the famous Dungeness crab in its home grounds. The road took us through a coastal flat full of salt-water farms, past hay baled and waiting, past cows chewing at a methodical two-beat, all underneath the wall of purple rock that we had just left behind.

In Dungeness we found one bar which served crab over the counter with draft beer. I found that it was nothing extraordinary as crab goes. I asked the barmaid (a real barmaid with rolled sleeves and dimples in her elbows) if the crab had been recently caught.

"The crab, sonny," she said, "is flown in from Canada, frozen."

And so it was I learned that, signs to the contrary, the tourist cannot buy Dungeness crab in Dungeness before September, when the commercial season begins. You can, if you have the time, bring your own rake, wade out over the sand flats and take six crabs by searching in the right places; you can take this catch, throw it in a pot with sea water and boil about twenty minutes and there you will have Dungeness crab—in Dungeness. Alas, our schedule didn't permit us the time.

En route back to Port Angeles, we saw a yacht bound for the San Juans, trailing a dark, peaceful wake line against the now-calm strait, reminding us that we had our own yacht waiting, ready to take us north as soon as we could get under way.

# 4

## *Bounteous B. C.*

ONCE BACK in Victoria, the most logical course is a return to the British Columbia mainland via Nanaimo. An early start from Victoria is advisable. The Juan de Fuca is liable to be most civil in the slack winds of early morning.

On the fifth day of the cruise we rose early and got the report that the strait was complacent. We slipped around the southern edge of the island and started the 65-mile leg north along the shore to Nanaimo, the beginning of the real run north.

We had had just enough time under way to get used to the shape of life aboard. A 24-foot cabin cruiser, such as the Norseman, is as roomy as an auxiliary sailboat twice the length. We had a good 8-foot beam all the way aft. Inside, the cabin was light and airy, thanks to the 2-foot-high windows on both sides.

The stove, icebox, and sink took up one side of the cabin, together with the usual unconscionably small w.c. that is standard cruising torture. On the other side was a table that made up into a double bunk; forward there were two bunks with feet that met in the forepeak; under all the bunks were huge accessible storage bins.

On a wall shelf over the sink, our cups and dishes (unbreakable Melmac) and silverware were strapped in place. The icebox was filled with Tupperware, airtight plastic containers that kept vegetables, bread and meat fresh. There was even a smart little Tupperware cylinder that preserved shelled raw eggs beyond the normal life of eggs in a refrigerator. (Banks developed a special skill for pouring six eggs out onto the skillet without breaking a yoke—on a good day.)

Behind the cabin, and bigger than it, was the cockpit, a 7- by 8-foot ballroom with helmsman's seat by the wheel to starboard. The rest of the cockpit was free of fixed gear. We had deck chairs (most of the time the chop was too heavy to sit in them), fishing rods, a small outboard for the dinghy, and a pair of water skis. Behind the cockpit the motors sat in a transom box, a 3- by 8-foot bin with room for the engineer, Portrey, to make repairs while under way. The ship's dinghy rested on the transom lid. Beside the helm was Portrey's special electric razor outlet.

On this, our fifth day out, we came piping into Nanaimo at 9 A.M., 64-miles in two hours and ten minutes. We debarked, each with a shopping list of second-thought items. This is the last large town (pop. 12,705) for nearly 500 miles on the route.

If you skip Victoria and the Olympic Mountains, you still have reason to come through Nanaimo from the San Juans: the port is on the most protected route and, besides, is the best customs port available. The customs office is right over the docks, in the Federal building. An outside phone near the docks permits you to call the late-duty customs officer if you should come to Nanaimo after 5 P.M. (His name is posted in the Federal building entryway.) It is possible to go through customs in Nanaimo at any hour of the day or evening without delay.

Nanaimo's stores and marine supply houses are excellent. We came back aboard stocked with edibles, spare line, and Scotch bought for $5.45 a fifth, and beer at $2.40 a case. We stowed it all quickly and moved out for the crossing of the Strait of Georgia, the body of water that here separates Vancouver Island from Pender Harbor on the mainland. We were hoping to pick up a couple of salmon before the evening was out: Pender has a reputation for giving up some prodigious fish.

It is only 20 miles or so to Pender Harbor. It has excellent shelter but, if the waves are cresting on the strait, it is a good idea to wait for morning. The cruise is still too young to risk shaking up the crew for the sake of a schedule. In early morning, the strait usually is passably calm. We ran across on a glass-smooth day in under an hour. The radio had informed us that we were just ahead of an expected blow and the blow came on as we got out of the strait, demonstrating one advantage of a fast boat.

The harbor mouth is first apparent as a gap in the line of rolling hills. Then it widens as you go in, opening on a large interior bay. There are several islands,

BELLA BELLA

RIVERS
INLET

CALVERT ISLAND

DUNCANBY LANDING

N
RLOTTE
ND

PHILLIPS ARM

STUART ISLAND

ALERT BAY

JOHNSTONE

STRAIT

PRINCESS
LOUISA
INLET

CAMPBELL
RIVER

VANCOUVER ISLAND

PENDER HARBOR

STRAIT OF GEORGIA

VANCOUVER

BIG SUCIA

BELLINGHAM

NANAIMO

SAN
JUAN
ISLANDS

CANADA

U.S.A.

VICTORIA

MAIN ROUTE ●

SIDE TRIPS ●

PORT
ANGELES

★ SEATTLE

HURRICANE
RIDGE

OLYMPIC PENINSULA

PUGET SOUND

WASHINGTON

The author water-skiing at Pender Harbor.

three sets of wharves and a tavern where, Banks swore, the finest Canadian beer was on tap.

We docked, gassed and went up to the tavern.

Taverns in British Columbia are divided into three parts. There is a first room in which women and their escorts are served. Then there is another in which men only are served. In the third room, lunch is served. Unescorted women have no room at all, unescorted men are not served with escorted women, and no drinks are served with lunch. It's like that.

Unescorted and without prospects, we bleakly drank our beer in the men-only room.

There were several daylight hours left before the salmon fishing would be good, so we tried out the water skis. The skis, I think, had been brought along as a sort of hazing for the Easterner, and I decided to rise or sink to the challenge here, rather than farther north. Portrey backed the Norseman around and pulled me off the wharf in great style. We swung around several islands without incident until I tried skiing on a single ski. Portrey cut across our own wake and I failed to. The water was at a temperature that quickly drained one's will to swim. By the time Portrey and Banks picked me up I had had enough and I got down in the cabin to change rapidly into warm clothes.

When I came back on deck, Portrey, topping off a Pepsi, said that he was about to go look for a herring ball. In Maine, where I have cruised, local fishermen invent a flock of "sand shrike" to mystify outsiders, so I viewed the notion of a "herring ball" with suspicion. Portrey patiently explained that a school of herring will form a ball at the approach of the dog shark, thousands upon thousands of herring all packing into a tight round glob. They pack so tightly, Portrey said, that the result is too big and hard for the dogfish to swallow. It can become an offensive weapon as well: the herring have been known to pack around a dog shark so tightly he cannot move.

This herring ball, with or without dog shark, tends to float toward the surface: the gulls pile up over the ball in a great, white tower of birds, flying up to dive on the herring. A fisherman who spots the gulls can run to the place and there, like a great silver basketball, are the herring. One dip and you have a thousand bait.

What happens to the dog shark? Portrey didn't say. He went off on another tack.

He said we could get our own bait by jigging rather than buying herring at one of the wharves. As it was a little early for herring balls, Portrey said we had better start jigging. He said that he had twenty hooks on a line and that was all we would need. Just hooks. The shine off the hooks, Portrey said, looked like plankton, and the herring come at it. A little jerk on the hooks and up come the herring.

We tried it. I watched while Portrey maneuvered us out to the mouth of the inlet and Banks, on the bow, started to jig the line up and down. Up came three shining herring, flapping each on its hook. A bit of this and we had a pailful of bait. I am still not sure about the herring ball.

We baited up and started trolling, circling back and forth until sunset. We caught no salmon in the evening's outing, but I did catch an outraged rock cod. He came up, spines splayed out and gills extended in quivering exasperation. We returned him, but several of his cousins got our remaining reserve bait. Portrey went out on the bow jigging for more while we continued to trail three lines from the poles in their holsters astern. I steered and Banks hotted up some coals in a small charcoal grill outside the cabin door. He laid three steaks on, put a pot of corn-on-the-cob atop the alcohol stove and waited. We moved gently around in the soft evening, redolent of good food and good living. The gulls flew in and out in long glides, spotted against the green of steep hills that rose out of the bay. We chugged along until the steak was turned and salted, then pulled the lines in, cut the motor and drifted in silence. To the west, the sun sank over Vancouver Island and silvered the passage in between.

The next day, after a breakfast consummated with a Canadian beer, we steered out of the harbor and turned due north, inland along Jervis Inlet. We had decided to take in one of the most-visited spots along the coast, the roaring falls of Princess Louisa Inlet, located at the end of the multiple reaches of the Jervis.

As we went in along the reaches, a strange and wonderful transformation took place. Here is heaven or what must pass for it among cruising yachtsmen: mile after mile of mountains climbing out of ocean, rock wall going six, seven, eight thousand feet straight up, finally, to snow caps. There are hills, foothills, mountains and giant mountains. Jutting inland all along the coast north of Pender are reaches, passages, and arms that slice as much as 60 miles into the mainland,

The high walls of the Royal Reaches, Jervis Inlet. →

North of Pender Harbor the mountains begin to billow up from the sea.

winding in and out and around like a giant's Venice. Sometimes you sail in your own private labyrinth, sometimes run with a fishing boat or two, sometimes steam along with three or four fellow cruising rigs—outboards, inboards, auxiliaries—bow waves splashing white against the walls of slate-gray rock on either side.

The sheer walls are powdered with lichen at the dark tide mark. Here the first small green trees cling precariously; next the first large evergreens hang tenaciously from the rock, leaning out and then straightening into 50- and 60-foot trunks; beyond the first rank is another rank and then rank after rank ascending to the dark tips lined against the sky on the cloud-scraping backbone of the shore.

The whole coast is carved from rock, cut so irregularly that it is more of a network than a shore line. Add to this the myriad islands, and you have a jungle of canals and passages, true Inside Passage country.

One cannot cruise these waters without becoming interested in their past history—not the geologic past but the human one. The Spaniards came to this shore once and they were followed by the Russians, the British, and the Americans. Many great square-rigged ships sailed round and round in here, putting out long boats, sending parties exploring inland along the arms, along the rivers, and over the portages. At the end they all were turned back by the mountains. Their search was not for gold or furs, but for the great mythical river, that fabulous River of the West that was to run from Hudson's Bay—a long, long river whose discovery would enrich beyond belief the discoverer because he would have claim to the Northwest Passage, the sea road to the riches of the Orient.

### SIDE TRIP TO PRINCESS LOUISA INLET

Our hull ran through the Prince of Wales, the first of the Jervis reaches. The walls climbed higher on both sides. We turned into the Princess Royal Reach where the walls came closer, and into Queen's Reach, narrower yet; some 40 miles inland, we spotted the island that hides the clefted entrance to Princess Louisa Inlet. Just behind the island, the Malibu Rapid floods out of Princess Louisa. It was a sluicing tide that drummed against the hull at 10 knots. We cleared the rapids and turned left to tie up at a float belonging to the Malibu Club, a boys' camp. We got permission to climb the shoulder of the entrance. Portrey took the Norseman out into the rapids again. Banks and I climbed. We got out on the cantilevered front porch of the Malibu Club and shot the Norseman skipping up the white-flecked tide run 150 feet below, a tiny yellow toy cruiser.

Going toward Chatterbox Falls.

We had to buck a 7-knot tide to reach the end of the arm. Once around the first corner, we could see the snow-capped peaks with the tenuous strings of snow melt skidding down the face of the wall at the head of Princess Louisa Inlet. The stream swells as it runs toward the bottom of the wall for its great, arching leap over the edge into the sea. It was a formidable cataract, thundering against the whine of our motors. The falls crash into the tidewater from the tops of the trees, a spectacle that makes the name, Chatterbox Falls, a misnomer.

There are docking facilities next to the falls: a narrow floating walkway tied between log booms. We tied up and walked toward the white spout that came roaring into the sea, turning the water to milk. Portrey stayed behind to helm the Norseman into position for photographing it from above the falls. Banks and I went into the dense forest and up the trail that parallels the stream. The wind from the rush of water blew clouds of droplets across the path. It was a wet, misty walk.

We worked our way up the 60-degree incline, swearing at the wet rock. After ten minutes, we made it out onto the stream above the falls. The water comes past the banks as if shot from a fire hose, bouncing 6 to 8 feet over small rocks, finally making that grand lunge to the surface of the arm, 200 feet below. The rock along the stream was slippery as an eel's back. We kept as far away from the stream as the woods permitted. Once a piece of moss underfoot gave way and I sat precipitously, but recovered with nothing worse than palpitations. A loose rock, weighing 20 pounds, which we threw into the stream, was hosed over the brink without a pause. A human body would likewise be catapulted over the edge seconds after it fell in.

We skinned across a log over the stream and set up our cameras. Portrey brought the Norseman out by the foot of the falls; we photographed it cruising about among the other boats far below, wreathed in the dancing filaments of bouncing water at the top of the falls.

Back at sea level, we stopped to talk with a white-haired, barrel-chested man, brown as a bear and built like one: J. F. MacDonald, "Mac" of Chatterbox. He lives in a houseboat at the foot of the falls and claims an oldest resident's right to buttonhole visitors. He had once deeded all the land around the falls to the province for the perpetual use of yachtsmen. Mac retired when he was thirty-eight

The author skins across the falls to get a better camera position. →

and intends to stay retired. "People are naturally happy and lazy," he said, "and now with the industrial age on, we have gotten away from that natural feeling. In my lifetime things have changed so much that we need to restore the balance. And that's what I'm doing. I am restoring the balance. I can use lots of help."

Doomed to imbalance, we steered out toward the mouth of Princess Louisa, whence we had come. By mid-afternoon we had left Jervis and headed for Stuart Island, 85 miles away.

# 5

## *To the Salmon Grounds*

OUR CRUISE PLAN called for a straight run to Stuart Island. The protected route to Stuart makes it an ideal landfall for the yachtsman heading north from Jervis. Stuart is a good base for operations in this part of the Inside Passage. From here, we intended to cruise to Phillips Arm and to Campbell River, both salmon-fishing grounds. We were to cruise Phillips first and then the protected route to Campbell via Stuart Island and across the island maze to Campbell River. (These islands are only sketchily indicated in the accompanying map.)

The cruising possibilities here are as great as those of the San Juan Islands. Phillips Arm, for instance, is a fine 30-mile reach and has an explorable river at its end. Many people spend an entire two-week vacation cruise in this area, exploring, finding snug coves and anchorages, cooking ashore and getting a tan.

On our way to Stuart, we ran past one of the world's biggest pulp mills at Powell River, a startling and incongruous complex in the wilds. We plunged into the maze then, and Portrey was kept busy paging the marine atlas, muttering island names and course numbers to himself. We reached Stuart at six, after a four-hour run from Chatterbox Falls.

Stuart itself is a fishing fleet depot. It has a good general store. Like all depot stores, this one has dry goods of a limited sort and an adequate grocery counter, but is usually a bit short on milk and eggs.

At wharfside there were trawlers with outrigger poles like pairs of giant buggy whips over each hull; there were gill netters, their stern drums filled to the rim with seines; and purse seiners with mast and boom poised. Some hulls were 40-footers with deep freeze and others 20-footers run by lone, rugged Canadians. Some fifteen thousand Canadian fishermen work this coast. Their fleets spread like chaff all up and down it. In a country where the hulls get fewer and fewer as you go north, the presence of the fleet provides a welcome safety factor. In addition, there is a watchdog fleet of government boats on hand to keep navigation marks set, to regulate the fishing fleet so that all get a fair share, and to keep sport fishermen from depleting the schools illegally.

At Stuart, I stopped by a boat that was being single-handed by a wiry looking old fellow with a slight Scot's burr and a canny face set off by one pale blue and one dark blue eye peering out under dense brows. He was a trawler man and lived on his boat, a 20-footer with midships cabin containing motor, gear and a board bunk. He had a set of four 20-foot poles, mounted in holders, all equipped with steel lines. The line on any pole can be attached to a winch drum. The drum connects to the engine, and when the drum is put into gear, any salmon on the line is hauled up to the boat willy-nilly. The trawling man's line is weighted with a 25- to 40-pound lead ball; on each line there are three to five spring snaps. The snaps secure nylon leaders, 6 to 70 feet long, ending in a hook.

The old Scot favored the long leader. "When they hit," he said, fixing me with his light eye, "this salmon goes straight on, like a freight train. He goes 50 feet before he quits. If he hits the end of a leader before that, he tears something loose. If he stops by himself, he just fights the hook. He sees it's no use going ahead. When I wind him up and get my hand on the leader, if he still wants to fight, I unhook the leader and snap it onto the stern until he gets tired of it.

"I'm hoping to boat a thousand silver this year. At three dollars a silver, I can almost make my new outfit this year. I fish north from here where they run 8, 10 pounds. That's where the money is. Figuring by the moon, they'll be here in two or three days. Then we start making money. Right now, we're just making expenses.

"Stay away from Campbell River. That's where the tyee run. An ill-behaved fish. He'll run back and forth, around, ahead of you and before you get him in, he has every hook on your rig in him and there'll be three hours spent unwrapping them."

By this time, Portrey, over in the Norseman, was making gestures to indicate that he had the sausage done to a turn. We went early to bed, planning to assault the Phillips Arm salmon massively in the morning.

## SIDE TRIP TO PHILLIPS ARM

At dawn on the seventh day of our cruise we crept quietly out of Stuart and into the entrance of Phillips Arm. The arm itself cut 30 miles inland, between walls that reared half a mile high, supporting Canadian sky between them. We ran steadily until we came to the great river at the head of the arm, where the salmon were drawing as their time neared.

The commercial fishermen are kept out. Phillips is a pleasure-fisherman's lake. After rounding the last bend, you idle into a mooring boom near cribs in which logs lie awash, ready for the lumber-mill tugs. The Fisheries Commission boat ties up here. You have to board this boat to sign for your license (each arm has its own limit). The license is free, but you have an obligation to report your catch to the commission. It can tally the take yearly from Phillips Arm. The Fisheries man said that 1,000 yachts checked in to Phillips Arm last year, and 300 salmon were taken on lines (only about half of the boats fish).

The Commission boat was a typical Canadian yacht with cabins strung out along the long deck like attached dwellings. The Fisheries man and his wife live aboard. He takes a tour in his outboard once in a while, but he's on hand in the morning to weigh your catch. He said the record catch for the arm was a 78-pound spring (called king or Chinook salmon in the United States) and that last year his wife caught a 50-pounder. He showed us a shot of his wife holding the fish, and the fish was considerably taller than their two children alongside it.

"We had a man lose his line last week," he said. "He had a lot of line out, and, before the brake held, the salmon had run out the rest. But he wasn't as bad off as the man who was here the week before. The poor fellow had been fishing for three hours with no luck when he laid his pole in the boat to light a cigarette. And don't you know, a salmon hit it and yanked the pole right out of the boat." The Fisheries man added that if you don't like the salmon fishing here, you can take your fly rod in the dinghy and cast up the river; 2 miles up, in the shallows, there are cutthroat and steelhead biting well at this time of year.

We started trolling around ten, with three glass rods—as big around as a man's thumb—sticking into the rod holders, 6-ounce lead sinker on a 60-pound test Monel steel line, 40-pound test nylon leader, a big 5-inch spoon tied to each, a

In Phillips Arm, Banks pays out line as we start our first serious salmon fishing.

hook the size of a small gaff on the spoon. We were looking for fish, not light tackle records. For a considerable time, it seemed that we would get neither. I spent hours typing notes in the cabin below, an activity possible only when the Norseman was at trolling speed. The other two took turns at the wheel, crossing and re-crossing the grounds. At lunch, Portrey made his big, special two-hand bologna sandwiches. We puttered slowly and patiently up and down the lichen-spotted walls at the head of the arm. Finally, we hooked a small jack salmon. The jack is a sexually precocious spring salmon; it runs up the river after no more than two years in salt water, instead of the usual four or five and, actually, is the tenderest salmon morsel you can catch.

The sun started down and there was a faint trace of white moon. Then came a snarl and a whine astern. The center rod bent double. Portrey was at the rod before I had half risen. I got on deck as Banks furiously wound in one slack line; Portrey set the fish with a swing. I reeled in the other line; Portrey shoved the violently vibrating rod with salmon attached into my hands. "Take him," said Portrey, "because he's on."

*48*

He was. This was no jack. I pulled the tip high, dropped it, and reeled to start him in. Again—pull up, drop and reel. I pumped and he pulled back steadily. "Hope he's not so small we have to throw him back," said Portrey, grinning from ear to ear. After ten minutes, the sinker came to the surface. There was a black whirl on the water and the line screamed off the reel. We had seen him and he us. Ten minutes more of hard work and I had him back. Portrey slid the gaff into the water and said, "Oh, he's just a baby." But baby took off again as determined as the first time. By the time I'd bent over the rod long enough to bring him into range again, I was fervently hoping Portrey would gaff, but the fish was not ready. He sounded, straight down. Portrey was shaking his head and saying that it was almost a shame to gaff that poor little fish. I brought the fish to the boat once more.

Portrey, bent over the side, straightened up and the fish came up with him. For a moment there, man and fish were face to face with the fish shaking Portrey and Portrey hanging onto the fish. I wanted to drop the rod and help, it seemed even-up, but Portrey somehow managed to hoist the fish over the side. How could he have lifted such a monster? Well for one thing, because the fish weighed only 24 pounds. Portrey and Banks, stood in one corner of the cockpit, cramped with silent laughter. I stood up, trying to look nonchalant and failing.

Portrey and Banks went below, sobered up on a couple of Pepsis, and we went back to fishing.

Once more we had a strike in the night: the screech was horrendous. The strike ripped the line off the spool, and when Portrey set the brake the fish kept going, tackle and all. In our minds we all saw a $78\frac{1}{2}$-pound giant making off with our spoon and leader in the murk below.

The next morning we got the fish weighed in at the Commission boat, 24.4 pounds exactly, 37 inches long—and a girl, with two full pockets of roe. The brown hue indicated that it had been about two weeks in the inlet waiting for the stream to freshen and rise. The weight, pound for pound, is the best fighting weight of the salmon. It was a first-run fish. It had come back from the sea to spawn in its home river at the end of the normal period. Some of the springs seem to pass up the first four- or five-year rendezvous and come back instead at the end of six. These are the record fish that run up in the 75-pound range.

The Fisheries man gave us a little rundown on salmon weights: spring, 15 pounds average, 25, good; coho or silver, 8 to 9; hook-nosed silver, 15 or rarely,

Salmon fishing means hours of trolling back and forth along the shore.

Strike! and the hooked salmon charges along the surface like a little torpedo boat.

I boat the beast and pose for the traditional victory shot of angler and angled.

20; dog salmon, 7 to 10; humpy or humpback, or pink, 8 to 10; sockeye, the commercial salmon, almost never takes a lure but averages 5 to 7 pounds.

From this point inside Phillips Arm, the yachtsman has the choice of going over to Campbell River for fish or of heading straight up the Passage for Alert Bay, the jumping-off point for the northern British Columbia coast. Campbell River has supplies, marine stores (Campbell River is a town, not a depot), the famous Tyee Club and the fabled Tyee Club sand bar and its larger, harder-fighting tyee salmon, colorful saloons, the fishing fleet, a movie house—supported by the fleet—and a salmon smokery where your salmon can be seasoned, smoked and tinned.

The scenery, on the other hand, does not compare with the country around Stuart Island. Overnighting at Campbell River means rising with the fleet at approximately dawn. When the motors start up, sleep is impossible.

On the balance, we decided to visit Campbell, partly because we had an invitation to visit Roderick Haig-Brown, the noted salmon authority, to talk fishing with him. Haig-Brown, besides being an internationally celebrated writer, is a salmon and steelhead fishing man par excellence, and a Knight of the Empire.

### SIDE TRIP TO CAMPBELL RIVER

The best way to get to Campbell River via protected water is to run Nodales, Discovery, Seymour Narrows and Campbell Passage between the islands. This was our route. A light chop sprang up at Nodales and cut our speed to 20 mph. I balanced against the tilting platform of the cockpit deck and gloomily thought about the Americans aboard *Gee-Bee*, a 65-footer out of Portland, Ore. We had hailed them on the way out of Phillips Arm. I wished that we had not—they had just been to Alaska and were on their way back because it had rained up there for two solid weeks.

At 12:30 we came into Seymour Narrows, formerly the site of an obstacle known as Ripple Rock. The tides here were such that they tended to carry ships right onto Ripple. The bottom is sown with wrecks. But Ripple no longer is dangerous. The Canadian government bored into the rock by tunneling from the shore, laid enough explosive in Ripple to rip it off the charts and touched the explosion off.

In Seymour Narrows, bluffs of buff and orange to starboard were backed by sloping hills; behind the hills lay a white, dark-edged cloud. In our path, gulls

52

hove on to the chop like a small white fleet; a black duck came spinning off the wave tops, barely clearing the crests. At 12:45 we passed the Elk Falls paper mill, seen as a single tall stack over great flesh-colored piles of pulp chips.

We came into Campbell River in midafternoon. We were to visit Sir Roderick, stock up on supplies and, in the morning, go out on the famous tyee waters to try our luck. Campbell River starts on a bar-lined sea-front street; the town then moves up away from the sea and becomes more respectable. The waterfront wharves are jammed with fishing boats, and the bars with fishermen. The taxi service is excellent: fishermen are notoriously loath to walk.

We caught a taxi and went straight off to Haig-Brown's, on the very bank of the Campbell River. It flows through Sir Roderick's yard and down to the sea just north of town. Sir Roderick offered us Scotch and talked fishing while the Campbell outside gleamed and glinted through big windows, lighting up rows of books, floor to ceiling. Roderick, tall and spare and mild, managed to tell us a good bit about the Oncherynchus, the Pacific salmon, during dinner. There are, he said, five of them, broadly speaking, and the largest and grandest are the spring. When a spring over 30 pounds is caught off Campbell River, he is called by his Indian name: tyee. Residents of Campbell River and the members of the famous Tyee Club whose headquarters are located on a sandspit at the mouth of the river all believe that the tyee is not just a spring but has a distinction in fighting spirit. (Ichthyologists disagree.) The light on the Campbell River outside was dim when we took our leave.

What does one do in the evening at Campbell River? Not much if one wants to rise at dawn and fish with a clear head. We sampled a few bars and then went to the movies. The show was "Doctor's Dilemma," from the Shaw play. The audience was full of by-God fishermen and I believe the fact that we had washed and shaved for the visit to Haig-Brown's went unappreciated here. The film had a punch line much repeated by one of Shaw's doctor-charlatans: "I believe we must stimulate his phagocytes." The phrase became a standard exclamation during the cruise.

Fishing at Campbell River is, largely speaking, divided between the haves and the have-nots. The haves have a rowboat and can therefore fish in the crowded waters off the Tyee Club sandspit, either hiring local guides to row them or rowing their own skiffs. The have-nots, ironically, are people like us with a big cruiser on our hands. Have-nots fish in the Campbell channel, since they would not be welcomed by the rowboat fleet in the waters off the sandspit.

The next day, before we tried our luck at the tyee, we motored to the famous sandspit, staying out of the way of the rowboat fleet that was scuttling about on the channel side. The Tyee Club stood in the center of the spit, a low nondescript building of weathered shingles surrounded by tents pitched on the grounds by fishing parties. The club has the deceptive simplicity of many famous rendezvous. A watchman let us inside under close supervision, and we found the walls hung with old, worn photos of giant fish beside their captors. The largest fish went $70\frac{1}{2}$ pounds and the largest fisherman well over 200. For the rest, the furnishings could have been those of any low-rent summer cottage.

The coveted Tyee Club membership comes with catching a fish above a certain size. The prospective member will spend at least three or four days a season trying to make the club, hunched over his rod in the rowboat, being rowed endlessly back and forth by his guide, and paying $50 or $60 a day for the privilege. When the tyee really run, the little strip of favored water is alive with rowboats. Every tyee man prays fervently at such times that now the guide will soon have him in the right spot to hook a gold membership (60-pound fish) or a ruby membership (70-pound fish) in the club.

We made off for Campbell Channel where we spent the morning fishing for tyee that did not bite. We gave it about four hours. During this period, our phagocytes were very quiet. If you have better luck than we did, the harbor master can arrange to have your catch smoked, tinned and shipped to the States (35 cents a pound plus postage) so that you can serve up your own salmon at a cocktail party (a delicious triumph) as hors d'oeuvres.

From Campbell River the yachtsman can go north to Queen Charlotte Sound and cross to the second section of the Inside Passage, upper British Columbia. Or he can content himself with keeping to the islands and channels of Georgia Strait until his vacation is over. The run to Queen Charlotte up Johnstone Strait is likely to be rough and the Charlotte itself is almost bound to be. The yachtsman with less than a keen desire to explore upward and onward is best off south of Queen Charlotte. A yachtsman with no more than two weeks at his disposal should stay south in any case. Queen Charlotte can go bad for two, three or four days at a time, putting any urgent return trip in jeopardy. Generally speaking, Charlotte Sound is the dividing line between the two-week vacation and longer ones.

We had twenty-one days left to us—plenty of time to make Juneau and come back again. We started off. The Norseman cut through the wave tops and bounced off to the beginning of Johnstone Strait, the first gauntlet between us and upper British Columbia. Beyond was our port for the night: Alert Bay. At Alert, we would be 300 of the 800 air miles to Juneau. At 12:15 we swung out of Discovery Channel around Chatham Light and we were at the mercy of the Johnstone, a stretch that, nine days out of ten, provides a rough five- to eight-hour haul against a vicious sea. Today was one of the nine. The prevailing westerly and the strong-running tide had combined to form the famous Johnstone "square wave," not high, but potent. The square wave sometimes separates the men from the boats. As we pounded along, Banks noted that the Johnstone was famous for knocking the bottom out of cruising yachts.

# 6

## *Across the Big Open Water*

AT FIRST we went bucketing along through the neck-jerking, bottom-basting chop of the Johnstone at 25 mph. Then the waves got squarer and we came down to 15 or so, and then 10. The chop was building and the spray breaking back over the bow, spattering thick salt on the windshield. We came down to 7. All of us were by then holding onto whatever we could reach. The waves were easily 3 feet high and no more than 6 feet apart.

A providential tug came steaming up astern, going for a load of timber. We hopped gratefully behind and let the tug take the brunt as far as Havannah Channel. We scooted into Havannah and began a faster pace on this longer, but calmer, detour route. We took Havannah north and Clio west, and, finally, came back to the Johnstone. Here the water was still rough. Portrey curved the Norseman into a small cove just off the Johnstone. He wanted to wait for a couple of hours to see if the waves wouldn't quiet down. We made our evening meal: the jack salmon that we had iced down at Phillips Arm. It went nicely with canned corn and fresh salad.

At 8 P.M. we were underway again. The Johnstone hadn't let up: it was a banging ride all the way to Alert Bay. Above us, the light was slowly dying in the soft contour of the evergreens; the sun was having its last glints off the fractured surface of the water. In the cabin, a pot rolled on the floor and I staggered below, stuffed the pot into the locker and slammed the locker door before it all came out. The sun, now behind us, threw the folds of the big hills into relief, hills folded like sleeping elephants. We passed a big Alaska liner, running smoothly over the stuff that was pitching us all about; the liner was the right size for this kind of sea. The passengers, on their way from Juneau to Seattle, stood at the rail and looked down at us. They had all the luxury of an ocean crossing and the scenery of a mountain climb. Would we have traded places? At that moment, I might have been willing—but not for long.

We hit Alert at 9 P.M. and pulled into the wharf. Alert Bay looks like a peaceful medium-sized fishing port. Then one becomes aware of the smell of violence from the bars and cheap restaurants that crowd the narrow streets. Soon one is convinced that a good war whoop could trigger a brawl that would involve every saloon on Main Street. The shack homes and false-front stores and the somewhat somber and sullen look of the people give the town a smoldering, raw feeling. Its men are just back from the sea, or down from the lumber camps or the mines, all eager to raise hell. Alert Bay probably is a fair approximation of the way the frontier towns of the American West were. It looks as though it could be murder.

We did not feel much disposed to challenge Alert Bay, having survived the Johnstone. Instead, we turned away from the unbuttoned part of town to inspect the justly famous "Totem Park," an area dedicated to the display of giant wood poles carved by the Northwest Indians. I found them eerie. The twisted faces piled one atop the other were sinister in the darkening shadows, the conjurations of a nightmare.

Late as it was, and tired as we were, we all well knew the need to push across Queen Charlotte Sound—if it could be done that night. We called the Coast Guard. They advised us that it had been blowing from the northwest for the better part of a week so that the waves on Queen Charlotte were big, and breaking. But they said also that the wind might ease toward morning.

At Queen Charlotte, when the weather says stop, you stop. The run to shelter at Duncanby Landing, near the mouth of Rivers Inlet, is 65 long miles. In a fast outboard, it is a rule of thumb that you should be able to make at least 15 knots to consider crossing. If you can't hold 15, then it is too rough. The winds can escalate rapidly here and you need time to get off before the going gets tougher, assuming that you started in a marginal situation in the first place.

Ounce for ounce, the modern cruising yacht, even a relatively light one such as the Norseman, is as resilient as a steel shell, and inherently stable. But once the Charlotte rollers start breaking strongly, the work of the helmsman becomes crucial to the safety of all: a yacht that takes a hard-breaking crest the wrong way can have a cockpit half full of water in a wink. The really large crest can cause a boat to broach and possibly turn turtle on the spot. This should not obscure the

57

fact that hundreds of hulls cross Queen Charlotte every year, skippered by experts and by not-so-experts. A bare half-dozen or so get into trouble through inexperience and impatience. If you are not a tough and tried salt-water cruising man, cross Queen Charlotte Sound in reasonable weather only.

We waited. We had plenty of company. There were ten or fifteen cruisers in the area just sitting it out in hope of a break in the weather. One had been there five days, but he was counted as overcautious. We took to our bunks. Portrey set the alarm for 2 A.M.

When the clock rang, Portrey got up and went ashore to phone the Coast Guard. He came back to report that the waves were breaking all over Queen Charlotte Sound. We went back to sleep. At 5:30, as far as we could tell, the wind had lightened. Portrey decided to go off immediately, without waiting to call. He had the canvas cover off the cockpit before I was out of the sleeping bag. He gunned the motors and off we went—no breakfast—for Duncanby Landing, over the ocean.

We rounded into the open water and found the waves were bounding and bouncing. We had to come down to 7 mph in a hurry. We scooted back with the northwester on our tail to take shelter at Malcolm Island, a somewhat shorter retreat than going all the way back to Alert Bay. There are several little holes-in-the-wall for cruisers who get chased off the Sound. (The most popular, next to Malcolm, is God's Pocket.)

About 10:30 the wind seemed to abate. We had a small meal and at 11:45 were off again. Conditions on the Sound were much better. We could just hold 15 mph. There was a slight drizzle and the hull climbed and fell on huge waves, but the size of the swells was not particularly bothersome. A nice big roller is much pleasanter than a small chop.

The sun came out and the wind freshened. We cleared the northern tip of Vancouver Island, far off to port. The island had stood between us and the Pacific for 282 miles and now we were on our own. We ran for Cape Caution on the mainland, course 306. The swell began to wrinkle with a nasty chop. Our speed went down a bit. Portrey, nevertheless, pushed for all he could, edging back up to speed whenever there was a respite in the steep rolling chop. Half an hour later we were moving along at somewhat better pace; Portrey was up to 20 mph. We had a good long look across the gray Pacific rolling toward Japan—but we were more interested in losing the view than in savoring it.

After three hours of rising and falling on Mother Ocean's billowing bosom, we had gotten well across. Off Pine Island, we were greeted by a committee of porpoises. They shot up to the stern with unbelievable bursts of speed—as if to tag us—and then fell away, playing. We were now making 25 mph, but this didn't bother the porpoises at all. They stayed with us like a salvo of tawny torpedoes, rolling up and blowing their breath in small steamy spurts before shooting away for good. Next, we ran into herring duck, setting them off in low trajectories, their bodies smacking through the wave tops to get out of the way. They were too full of herring to rise off the water. They gave up being birds and dived out of harm's way as soon as we closed with them.

Now the weather became less obliging. As we moved up the coast toward Duncanby Landing, the swell became covered with small hard-hitting waves; the sky grayed. The crests of the swells began to break slightly. To starboard, the sea met the bleached rock of the islets in grim white lines.

By 2 P.M. the waves had started to cap in earnest and we encountered our worst beating to date: I timed the waves and found that we were lurching over a wave and dropping smack on our underside exactly once every two seconds; every third or fourth drop was harder and rattled the crockery in the cabin seriously; every eighth or ninth produced a real smash that seemed to tear things loose inside. Finally, at a sea-stained rock about ten miles north of Cape Caution, we turned hard starboard. The rock told us that it was time for the ultimate run into Duncanby Landing. We were more than ready for what Duncanby had to offer: a welcome, clean, well-supplied fishing depot with gas and food aplenty. When we got there, we took our alcohol stove ashore and had the depot mechanic fix a leak that had been punched in it; there is nothing to bring on *mal de mer* quite as efficiently as the sickly smell of spilled alcohol. We provisioned and then we were off to the fishing up Rivers Inlet.

The main route of the cruise goes north from Duncanby, not east into Rivers. But the fishing at Rivers Inlet was one attraction that Portrey was determined not to miss. The alternative would have been to go twenty miles north to anchor in the shelter of Calvert Island and spend the next day on the Calvert beach. But we were for Rivers Inlet: if the fishing proved bad, we could take a ride up the river at the end. This is grizzly country ashore and the river usually yields a view of the famous silver-gray bear, down for a bit of fishing in his own way.

## SIDE TRIP TO RIVERS INLET

Once into Rivers, the yacht runs between canyonlike walls; 60 miles of this high rock brings you to the head of the inlet. Here the great salmon river rolls its opaque green water out over the heavier gray of the sea. If you are exploring or bear-watching, you go on up the river to a likely looking spot and anchor for the evening. If you are fishing, you check in at the small building in the cannery that stands a mile from the mouth of the river. The cannery is seasonal, deserted nine-tenths of the year, but the Fisheries Commission office is open all season long. After we checked in and obtained permits, we got back into the boat and hung out our lines.

But this was pretense—what we really wanted to do was sleep, after the past twenty-four hours. The fish obliged. Sundown found us in our sacks.

We started the eleventh day of our cruise at 8 A.M. To improve our luck we soaped down and had a dip in the brackish surface of the inlet. It is possible to bathe in this semi-fresh top layer of water, but, even though the water comes out of the river and not from the sea, it makes as cold a bath as I've had. That water is *icy*.

We had only been out for twenty minutes when we got our first strike. Banks, alone on deck, grabbed the rod and set the fish. Then, holding the rod in one hand, he reached for the wheel with the other to turn the boat. This was a salmon that you ran with, not against: the line was melting off the reel. In a matter of a second or two, the monster picked up speed so fast he brought the pole handle down against the dinghy with a loud crack—and was gone. (So was a patch of skin from Banks' right knuckle.)

At 11:10, we got another strike. This one stayed with us longer. He surfaced right away and made a tight half-circle around the stern, splitting the green surface with a trail of froth. He then charged like a miniature Moby Dick, the fore half of his 35 pounds almost clear of water. He dived under the hull at the last moment and came up on the other side; Portrey, frantic, stabbed the rod into the water astern to keep the line out of the prop blades, managed to clear the line, and swung the pole up on the other side. The salmon charged again, and this time, when he came up, he spit the spoon in a glittering arc and was free.

*60*

Going up Rivers Inlet after crossing the Queen Charlotte Strait.

At 1 P.M., Portrey said, "Get your cameras, boys, here they come."

And there they were, stiff glistening black club dorsal fins, sticking 5 feet into the air, veering and teetering across the water's surface: killer whales! One dorsal passed between us and shore, about 50 yards off. The killer whale surfaced, water cascading down the 30-foot length of a black back and black sides; the dead white

The club dorsal of a killer whale interrupts our pursuit of salmon.

The second killer whale surfaces to join the first.

marking of the midbody came into view and then a small, wicked-looking head; there was a hollow "Hahhh!" and the killer's exhalation steamed above its head; the head disappeared, the back rolled forward and down; all that was left was the club, shedding a crest of water. Then it, too, went slicing down out of sight.

A second later, another club dorsal surfaced, another animal arose, a dolphin-like head blew, and we heard the deep rush and saw the cloud of vapor. There were only four of them, but they seemed to be cutting up the whole bay with their restless lunges—roll, whoosh and down. Up, roll, down. Nothing about the way they went about their business invited us to join them for a swim. The killer whale is looking for salmon, yes, but especially for the warm-blooded seal. We felt that he would probably have failed to make the fine distinction between a human being and another similar-sized animal with more fur.

The killers moved off. We took after them, Portrey at the helm, Banks and I shooting film. The two of us sat braced on the foredeck, firing whenever the beasts rose. Finally, evading our best efforts to close in, the killers swam back the way they had come, with the same unhurried dip and roll.

Although there is no documented case of a killer-whale attack on human beings, there is plenty of ground for pessimism. A killer pack will tackle anything that moves in the sea, from bull walrus to a herd of whale. They have been known to splinter shelf ice for the purpose of dumping seals into the water. The killer whale torpedoes up from below, shatters the ice with his snout, and picks up his seal dinner.

Killers will go after other whales, wanting nothing else than the tongue. Part of the pack harries the whale while the rest crowd like leeches about the whale's mouth, waiting for the jaw to drop just a bit; then they tear the tongue from the animal in grisly teamwork. Is a boat in any danger? Probably not. Although the killer whale is substantially larger and heavier than most yachts, it seems to respect power craft.

Once killer whales move into an inlet, scooping salmon, the fishing is over. The springs move down out of the way and stay for a day or so. Only the sockeyes, blissful idiots, continue jumping and moving about. But sockeye will not take a lure, so we decided to run up the river. We might well spot a grizzly or two coming down to fish. The Norseman breasted the 10-knot current of the river until we came to the first pool. This seemed to be a good enough spot, so we sat down to lunch and waited.

Here were the seals the killers had been looking for—they swam about, black rubber-ball noses stuck in the air, craning their necks to look—big black bulging eyes filled with curiosity. Here, too, were flies—big, fat anxious deer flies. We killed 386, "not counting the probables." The flies bit like hopped-up mosquitoes, unsheathing a formidable proboscis from under the ugly white rings around the eyes. We stuffed paper into the cracks in the cabin door while we ate, but still they came crawling through, lusting for us.

The bears, alas, were not about and we didn't wait very long for them. However, this is the center of fine grizzly country. Had we taken time, we undoubtedly would have seen at least one grizzly sow with cubs move into the river and bite at the salmon. (The males, the largest grizzly, usually stay in the woods, taking their fish from the creeks.) The area is a prime ground for trophy grizzly. If you want to try for one, you apply to the Canadian Game Commission and get your bear-hunting license ($25) before the cruise begins. The British Columbia game laws also require you to employ an experienced guide. With license, guide, and luck you can have yourself a stuffable grizzly head from Rivers Inlet in fairly short order.

We were up at 6:30 the next day. So were the killer whales, rolling and blowing on the far side of the inlet. That quenched any fishing. We reported to the Fisheries Commission man that we had been done in by the killers, and then we went over to the cannery dock to fill up with water from the cannery's ever-flowing supply.

The yachtsman at Rivers has the following prospect: he can run 60 miles out, then 20 miles north to the beach at Calvert Island, an island of beauty, completely wild (no supplies); or he can go straight on to Bella Bella, a fishing depot (plenty of supplies), 60 miles north from the mouth of Rivers Inlet. There is nothing at Bella Bella of particular interest. The only good reason for picking this alternative is a haste to go north.

We had plenty of time for Calvert, for a go at crab catching and a day of beach rest. We headed out and were high-tailing it up the Inside Passage within the hour, with visions of a sea beach in our heads. As we ran, the entire British Columbia coast south to Charlotte Sound and north to Namu was visible in sparkling clarity. The passage became a corridor between rows of sharp-edged mountains in the sea. Later a sea mist rose, and the hills on both sides became dark blue cardboard outlines stacked against a dusty blue sky. The wind came up, blowing from the north. Small white-caps ran toward us in white companies, marching below ranks of evergreen that lined the shores. A bald eagle flew across the passage and settled heavily in a cedar.

## SIDE TRIP TO CALVERT ISLAND

At noon, we anchored well up the arm that bisects Calvert from the east. We unfurled our crab net, a contraption about the size of a basketball goal; it had ports so constructed that the crab could crawl in but not out. We baited with spoiled steak, and lowered the net to the bottom. Landing, we made for the other side of the island and the beach. It was a ¾-mile walk in a moss-hung forest. The trail ends at the edge of the Pacific on one of the world's more breath-taking coves:

The beach at Calvert Island.

a ring of sand, fine and clean, backed by a semi-circle of cedar; it opens seaward on a barrier of reefs and, beyond, the Pacific rolls slowly toward infinity.

We dropped into the sand to lie, belly-warm, for an hour. Then our explorative zest overcame our happy laziness. I investigated the structure of the kelp that lay splayed over the sand like green bullwhips. Kelp has tentacles at one end, rock-graspers; at the other, thick end, it has a grapefruit-size bulb that floats in the sun. Dried on the beach, kelp has the consistency of vulcanized rubber. Portrey cut one up and blew, Joshualike, through the bulb. He produced a lingering muted bellow, a primitive fog horn. Kelp grows in patches, some big enough and trouble-some enough to be marked on the charts. It can raise hell with a propeller. When you hear a sound like a buzz saw hitting a pine knot, you can be sure that you are into kelp. The technique is to throw the entangled engine into reverse, unwind the kelp and then click to forward again in three seconds flat without losing head-way.

Walking through the thick cedar and fir on our way back to the boat, we stopped to pick red huckleberry from eye-high bushes. We had three bags in twenty minutes. The cedar on Calvert is a small (70-foot-high) relative of the redwood. The cedar stand here was a characteristic rain forest, with moss edging the limbs to the length of a goodly beard. The coast has about 200 inches of rain-fall a season, which compares well with the Congo. In the dense part of the stand, the fine, webbed moss imparts a green luminescence to the air.

Back on board, we hauled the crab net to find three of the ugly fellows inside, their eyes wiggling on the end of stalks that collapsed sidewise into sockets. The crabs clung to the net, cantankerous, clacking sharply, making the curious scolding noise of the crab. They tried to stick their pointed forelegs into our fingers and made crafty swipes with their front claws to see if they could catch us and pinch us to death. We had them hot from the pot, with huckleberries sugared in milk from our last bottle.

CLARENCE STRAIT

BELL ISLAND

WALKER COVE

BEHM CANAL

KETCHIKAN

ALASKA
CANADA

DIXON ENTRANCE

PRINCE RUPERT

BRITISH COLUMBIA

QUEEN CHARLOTTE ISLANDS

LOWE INLET

BUTEDALE

MILBANKE
SOUND

BELLA BELLA

RIVERS
INLET

CALVERT ISLAND

DUNCANBY LANDING

QUEEN
CHARLOTTE
SOUND

# 7

## *Faster, Northward*

IT WAS the thirteenth day of the cruise, and the time had come to begin our run for Alaska in earnest. The schedule called for our reaching Prince Rupert, the last town in northern British Columbia, by the end of the fourteenth day. We got away early in the gray light from an overcast sky. Low white wreaths crowned the mountains to the east and calm water reflected quicksilver colors. We ran north, passing up Namu by consent, since Namu has a smelly fish-rendering plant that makes the town less than desirable as a stop-off. We went on to Bella Bella, a dock-town fishing depot. There was a huge plank plaza on which a marine-supply and grocery store sits. Back of the plaza lay gas drums, seines, and sprawled Indians. From here, it is an 85-mile run to the next supply point, Butedale, another dock town. In between, there is Milbanke Sound, 10 miles of open water.

There is one good side trip to be made en route. That is the Gull Chuck, just short of Milbanke. In late July the silver salmon are likely to be running. The silver sometimes can be teased to take a spoon in spawning season.

We headed for the Gull Chuck and arrived to find it alive with silvers, enormously excited by the feel of fresh water coming down the stream. A certain proportion of fresh water to salt would soon fire the positive biological trigger and the school would make for the river as one. In the meantime, the silvers danced on their tails. They were past taking food but they would occasionally snap at a lure in excitement or irritation. We hooked first one silver and then another. That was all, though. We fished the morning out with no more luck, even going so far as to try casting from shore.

We ran toward Milbanke Sound, but it was too choppy to make good speed,

A brief try at catching salmon from land: late afternoon in Gull Chuck.

so we circled back to protected water and anchored in a small harbor for the night, gambling on fair water in the morning. We pan-fried the silvers for dinner.

We were up at 6:30 and caught Milbanke Sound asleep. We ran its 10 miles at top speed. Well into the Mathieson Channel on the other side, we stopped to inspect a stranded wreck. It was the ghost of the passenger liner *North Star*, run up on this reef in her heyday and left there for lack of salvagers. It is now a beautiful rust-red skeleton, the plates weathered and colored intricately.

We were watching for reefs ourselves. This is one of the stretches with bothersome underwater problems. The Inside Passage has very few. Mathieson also is the first of the natural canals of the Inside Passage: narrow calm channels less than a hundred feet wide where the water lies like glass. Once past the reef-studded section, we ran at full throttle through this mirror water. The low-lying morning sun gleamed off jet-black, slick kelp rods. Our motors beat out a hum of synchronous contentment, and we split the channel with our line of white, running behind the mountains to Alaska.

The wreck of an Alaskan coast steamer in midstream warns us there are reefs about.

Portrey maneuvers carefully through a narrow channel in a ripping tide, near Butedale.

We had plenty of time in these conditions to take a detour through Griffin Pass, one of the channels that parallels the main route. Griffin has two "overfalls" marked on it; an overfall is a torrential tide-rush that forms an equivalent of a waterfall at a local narrowing of a channel. We wanted to have the fun of running up one overfall and down the other. Anyone with a bit of extra time and about 60 hp can play this game. However, the pass is not charted: no inboard should try it because of the vulnerability of the propeller shaft.

### SIDE TRIP TO GRIFFIN PASS

Griffin Pass splits off about halfway to Butedale: it is a twisty little channel (too small to show in detail on our map) that we traveled at automobile speeds except for an occasional bout with a kelp patch. Not many boats come through here: kelp lies across the entire canal in places.

Around a bend, we came upon the mid-channel island that provides the blocking effect needed to create an overfall. In the early morning, it was still dark behind this particular bend, and cool. The white foam of the overfall poured down from the far side of the island, 50 yards of whipping, white water. Portrey put the bow of the Norseman firmly into the foot of the fall. The boat nosed up at a wavering 6 or 7 knots, with the engines at full cruising throttle to do it. Portrey corrected quickly whenever the boiling rush turned the bow toward either shore. If we had been thrust into a sidewise position, we'd have had to go back to "Start" and begin over again. The white and mahoghany water rapped by us, making a potent thunder on the underside.

Five minutes and we were through, elevated onto the surface of a small and quiet pond. It was a hushed world here. We motored slowly while the herring duck fled before us, slapping the water alternately with one wing and the other, careening across the surface like tipsy egg beaters. We startled a family of duck, mother and three. A seal slit the surface with a silver streak and then dived.

At the far end of the calm water, the second overfall poured down from the pond: this is the division of the tide in Griffin. We beached the boat and looked over the 30 yards of wild, down-rushing stream: no rocks marred the run, so we let the hull drift into the top of the stretch and went bounding down to sea level like a toy.

Now we gunned for Butedale. Mountains perfect as pyramids lined the channel sides. At 9 A.M., we met the liner *Canadian Prince*, going south. At ten, we passed two unnamed arms to starboard, both leading to blue-black ridges, snow-dappled, far away in the interior.

At 10:30 we noticed an orange-red streak winding tenuously down the channel. We ran back and forth over it to see if we could slice it up and disturb its continuity—it stretched mile after mile—but we could not make a noticeable break in the thread of it. The ribbon of red is made up of microscopic algae called "red tide." The natives refrain from drinking or cooking with this water or eating shellfish taken in it. So should yachtsmen. The little red plants can cause serious intestinal poisoning.

Mountains slid by and the calm water held. We were hell-bent for the north past gulls sitting on the water, white flags for our passage. We got to Butedale at 11 A.M.

The town of Butedale is another plank-plaza fishing depot with handy gas and food supply. From Butedale, which has no attractions of its own, the choice is to go on to Prince Rupert in a hurry, or to take a break at Lowe Inlet, the best salmon-watching on the coast. Since we were well on schedule, we decided to break at Lowe: we could still make the 115 miles from Butedale to Rupert before dark. This is a stretch in which you can often make very good time. We gassed and were on our way in twenty minutes, ripping past the brown washboard water-fall north of Butedale at 30 mph. The engines were humming in perfect beat. The ripples swept under the hull with a "r-a-a-a-a" as we knifed up Graham Channel, throwing a lather into the green beard of trees.

## SIDE TRIP TO LOWE INLET

A little after noon we turned off the channel and went up the short arm to the head of Lowe Inlet. Here the Lowe River comes flashing into the terminal pool of the arm, falling like a rush from a rainspout, sliding over magnificent boulders in clear, hard torrents to its final, foaming collision with the sea.

As we pulled up by the fall, the bay was erupting fish: blue-black silver bodies bombarded the white, almost vertical current. The sockeye were raging up the main falls, up two smaller side falls, and up any little trickle that seemed to prom-ise a way to the top. They bucked bodily over wet rock, jack-knifing, flipping and sprawling.

We rowed the dinghy over to the fall and tied up next to a Fisheries Com-mission boat. Banks and I went ashore with loaded cameras. I knelt unsteadily on a rock and tried to frame the showering sockeye bodies, but a sockeye tail-walked over the rock I had pre-empted; he gave me a good wet fanning before he flipped by.

The sockeyes jumped in squads, the leap of one touching off the others' leaps. Simultaneously four and five bodies would fling through the air and disappear under the violent sluicing white of the fall; then they became half visible again as blurred shadowy forms spattering water to both sides, lashing desperately straight up the cascade, only to be washed back into the pool. Up again. And again. The tide was not high enough to let the sockeyes make it yet, but the sockeye weren't waiting. The interior mechanism had gone off, and from now on all it said was "up."

A whole pond full of exhausted fish lay at the bottom, fanning their tails slowly in anger, waiting for their strength to come again. I reached under a rock and barehanded a salmon easily. I could have tossed him to shore, but the Fisheries

Two salmon leap simultaneously, trying to best the white water of the Lowe River.

A salmon tries a flying leap over bare rock in its attempt to find a way up.

But lands flat on its side, out of its element and off its mark.

Commission man posted here would surely have done his duty—which is to discourage this kind of thing. (There is a later run of silver salmon in which the fisherman can take three salmon on a line in all legality.)

From Lowe Inlet, after a lunch by leaping salmon, we set out for our last port in British Columbia, Prince Rupert. We were looking forward to spending the night in a real indoor bed with hot and cold running water in the bathroom. The weather closed in. For the first time on the trip, we had serious, driving rain. The coast, through the sheets of wet, turned to a miserable-looking rock desert.

But Portrey negotiated the open stretch that lies before Prince Rupert without difficulty in spite of low visibility and we docked at the Prince Rupert Yacht Club. Stein Diderichson, the manager, was notably hospitable. There was no charge for our berth, and he filled our water and gas tanks while we made for the Hotel Savoy, the recommended hostelry in town. The town of Prince Rupert, reportedly the locus of 10,000 souls, looked half that size. It has one good restaurant, the Broadway. It is not exactly a wild town, but we didn't mind. We had come 240 miles on our fourteenth day of the trip. We slept.

# 8

## *Alaska: Totems, Sulphur, and Whale*

IN SPITE of the rain and the threat of more rain to the north, we began to develop an eager impatience to get to Alaska. The sensation was somewhat akin to that experienced by long-distance jet travelers in the last slow hour before arrival. It is a mixture of anticipatory excitement and mild apprehension that something somehow may go wrong at the last moment. It is a time when one's frustration threshold is likely to be low. Ours was.

The next day we checked out at Canadian customs, but the rain continued unabated and we were not so eager to dare the 86-mile run over the Dixon Entrance to Alaska in minimum conditions. The Dixon, the longest single open-water jump in the cruise, is only slightly less remarked for its big weather than Queen Charlotte. Nor was it only rain that held us in Prince Rupert. The wind was blowing, too, and the wind and rain combination was too much. (We knew we could take a bit of a chance and go, hoping to duck into Dundas Island's little harbor if the weather proved untenable, but none of us wanted that kind of an anchorage.)

Finally, at 1:30 P.M., we got a better report—wind slackening, water choppy but manageable, and more rain. It was good enough and we set off for Dixon Entrance. The foglike precipitation gave us a dead-reckoning navigation test which Banks passed with a good mark. As we approached Alaska, the sky cleared to pearl gray. At 3:45, out in the middle of Dixon Entrance, we crossed the border.

We had a brief moment of festive feeling: one of our main objectives—to get to Alaska in our own hull—had been achieved. We passed around a shot glass in the drizzle, and the rain came on stronger. The festive feeling died. "This will probably blow over in a month or two," said Banks. It was not quite a quip, because the rain can become a season up here, if you have bad luck. Rain seeped into the cabin from every crevice. The boat was shaking with seemingly uncontrolled ague brought on by the racking chop. Portrey did the only thing possible—pushed hard to get to Ketchikan before things got worse.

About 4 P.M., we saw the buildings of our first United States town since Port Angeles. We motored in, free of pounding at last, and tied at Ketchikan's wharves. The rain lifted as we got off the boat. The wharves were almost completely taken by pleasure and fishing fleets. We tied between two expensive-looking yachts out of Ketchikan and went to Customs to report in to the U.S.A.

Ketchikan, at first look, resembles the set for "Showdown at the O.K. Corral" mixed in with "Captains Courageous." The town is fronted by a huge plank plaza: the seiners bring in their 100-pound carcasses of gray-white halibut and hoist them onto the planks; the salmon fleet comes in to deliver its silver catch; booted fishing crews stride around like musketeers. Stevedores strain at tackle, men shovel fish-smelling crushed ice into storage bins. Behind all this, the town divides into 30 per cent bars, 30 per cent battered buildings and 30 per cent passable places of residence and commerce; the remaining 10 per cent consists of curio and gift shops.

There are welcome touches of the U.S.A.: a first-class hotel, the Ingersoll; air mail editions of the Seattle *Times* daily; a quick-service laundry; bartenders with fast small-talk; waitresses who kid; police who give friendly advice. (A Canadian town, by contrast, is stuffy—no women in the bars, no talking in the street, a subdued and quiet lot of citizens.) At its worst, Ketchikan seems right out of *Tobacco Road:* disgracefully shabby sections of waterfront; slums built over a dirty little riverlet (it used to yield a body a week); houses half empty, half gone, half lived-in. Cheek by jowl are the tourist emporiums selling walrus ivory, whale teeth and fur parkas.

We walked through this mixture of the raw and the touristy to the Ingersoll, and checked in. After a go-round with soap, we went out for a drink. We found bars full of hard-rock characters who chew and spit in the sawdust—lumberjacks, wharf men, and, as always, Indians, squat, friendly or slack-jawed, sulky.

We left the main part of town to walk up to the park and the totem-pole display there, one of the very best in Alaska: a collection of scowling, villainous, gleeful, rapacious, howling faces. In this part of the country, the totem carvers were from the Tlingit tribe, out of the Urals, Mongolia, and Siberia by way of the now-sunken land bridge between Siberia and Alaska. The tribe had developed, by the time they were first observed by the white man, a fairly serviceable and com-

Ketchikan clings to the side of a mountain, a city hanging half over the water.

plex social organization. It was contact with the whaling fleet of the Russians, however, that inspired pole-carving. The Indians took iron tools in exchange for pelts, and they took the masts on Russian ships as a form. Previously, totems had been carved on flat surfaces; now the art soared.

It reached its height in the late 1800's and then declined as the Northwest Indian was infected with white economics: trade pelt for liquor, drink the liquor. The missionaries did the rest of the job, encouraging a new social structure which did away with the old.

The old form of life had served to place the Northwest Indian securely on a ladder of social importance; his rung was clearly defined and his life's work fell within a given framework: there were slaves, a middle class, and there were chiefs. In the new way of life, all Indians had a place, too—at the bottom, below everyone white. As a result, the Alaskan integration problem is no less severe than that of the South.

The keystone of the old Indian economy was the potlatch. This was a feast and an economic conference all in one. It had no real relation to the present potlatch church social of the women's club variety. The Indian potlatch was a serious affair. Among other things, it was a ceremony at which the potlatch host, by giving objects of value, paid off all his old debts. His guests, receiving his gifts, contracted debts. All gifts had to be repaid twofold at some later date. Any chief, by giving a hell of a potlatch, could secure his old age and assure his sons of a start in the world. It was, in effect, a credit and interest system which placed considerably more wealth at the disposal of the society than the sum of existing material objects.

Poles were raised in commemoration of such a potlatch. The pole perpetuated the prestige of the potlatch giver, his potlatch, and his munificence.

The abstractions on a totem pole are sophisticated by modern standards of art. The pole consists of highly ritualistic carvings representing the great man's clan, his descent, and his feats. A shark on a totem pole is not a three-dimensional fish; it is shown as if slit down the back and spread, belly-up; the head is enormously enlarged, the eyes moved to the bottom of the head, and the gill slits expanded until they cover the whole body. The Indian used displacement and distortion for exact effect.

In the disruption of the clan, the totem carvers died out. The Indian society survived because its members were able to infiltrate white society to supply labor for the fishing and lumber industries. The more southerly Indian societies like those in the central United States were not even that lucky.

We spent an hour getting our land legs back, hiking up to the mountain walls that ring the town. (Everything that comes into Ketchikan comes by water or air.) Then we walked back to the Ingersoll and telephoned for reservations at the Narrows Club, 3 miles out of town, recommended as the best food and drink place in the area; it turned out to be a perfectly nice country club-like dining room with bar.

In the misty overcast of a new day, we collected our laundry, picked up a chunk of ice, and boarded our yacht. The yachting man in Ketchikan can push on and take the 170 miles to Petersburg immediately, thereby bringing the cruise toward a fairly rapid conclusion. Alternatively, he can stop off at Bell Island Hot Springs, 40 miles to the north. Bell Island lies on the Behm Canal; it offers cabin accommodations, mineral bath rejuvenation, and a high incidence of salmon.

We picked the latter and radioed for reservations. You can tie up at Bell Island and eat meals on your boat while you use Bell's mineral baths any time. However, to live and eat at the island's resort, one must radio ahead.

North of Ketchikan, the Norseman got into the open water of Clarence Strait; it was rough and the confused wave patterns were dusted by a chill Alaska rain. The wet bucketing hull seemed like a poor home just then, but at the end of 40 miles there would be a hot sulphur bath waiting at Bell; I had always wanted to stay at a spa.

## SIDE TRIP TO BELL ISLAND

Bell Island Hot Springs is unpretentious. It sits on the edge of the sea, over-looking a creek, surrounded by tall woods that seem to press upon it. When we saw it, the buildings had a lackadaisical charm; nothing was repaired too carefully; various owners through the years had decided not to spend too much on a place that the forest and the animals might repossess shortly.

The resort dining building has a lounge in fairly standard woodsy style. There are a number of subsidiary cabins strung out along the boardwalk trail parallel to the creek. Farthest from the sea is the bath house: here guests sit in zinc-lined tubs, absorbing the good (whatever it is) that comes from opening the pores to sulphur water. Bing Crosby and other rich yachtsmen and ordinary middle-class cruising men, too, have made this a stop for years on the Alaska run.

The stream beside the cabins was almost boiling with rainbow and Dolly Varden trout when we came slipping in to the small harbor at the creek mouth. We later took trout off the pier with the ease of five-year-olds hooking sunfish. (The only problem in fishing them was the million little black cod that insisted on hooking onto our lures.)

Our first move was to get a sulphur bath. The sulphur water is heated by the fires beneath the earth's crust; full of sulphurous compounds, it makes its way up to the surface by devious routes and, arriving at a temperature of 169 degrees, is trapped in a big cement well at the bath house. From there it is let into tubs inside. We each filled a tub, stripped, and, as directed, poured in an amount of cold water to bring the temperature down a bit; about fifty-fifty is the right mix, the proprietor told us. I believed. I mixed accordingly and sat down in the 6-foot tub with a splash. And got right up again. Good Lord, but it was hot!

In spite of the rain, the two others decided to go out for salmon in the afternoon. I opted for a nature stroll along the boardwalk. Out in the stream, an otter was cutting across—3 feet of slick, wet beastie. Gray loons were swimming and blue jays coasted to and fro over the boardwalk. The merganser, a red-headed duck, paddled about down by the docks. I saw a long arched back loping along the walk with a comic, stiff-legged, scared-cat gait: mink on the hoof, totally unaware of me and of the fact that he is considered a prime asset for high-class girls and society matrons.

There was a second mink, in the swim, heading downstream, an elongated cat that liked water. Mink will pry into anything that is left in the open at the boat dock: bait, bread, candy, and the contents of the sugar bowl—all go down a mink in a wink.

A tiny bird about the size of my thumb walked down the bank and disappeared into the water. The proprietor told me later that I had seen a water ouzel, a bit of a bird that has learned to hack around on the stream bottoms for marine grubs; the ouzel takes a deep breath and goes in. When he runs out of air, he comes out.

I moved back toward the cabin with the jays screaming at my head; up by the dining hall, the proprietor was pointing across the stream. I looked and saw two bears, Alaska browns, munching grass in the meadow. They stared us down, haughtily, then walked sedately back into the woods, leaving us our little footpath in the grassy cleft in the wilderness. Later on, Portrey and Banks came in, triumphant, with two salmon.

Next morning Portrey and Banks went out again and by lunch they had six more, bringing the fish total to eight: six medium-size spring, one humpy and one silver. We arranged to have the lot shipped back to Ketchikan and smoked for us. We would pick them up on the return trip.

At a lunch-time conference we agreed to go down the Behm Canal to Walker Cove, the most beautiful of the arms in this part of the Alaskan coast. It is a

Walker Cove: the most beautiful fjord on the Lower Alaskan Panhandle.

JUNEAU

ALASKA

TAKU RIVER

TAKU HARBOR

ALEXANDER
ARCHIPELAGO

STEPHENS PASSAGE

FORDS TERROR

LE CONTE GLACIER

PETERSBURG

CLARENCE STRAIT

BELL ISLAND

WALKER COVE

BEHM CANAL

KETCHIKAN

30-mile round trip, and in any tolerable weather it can be counted on for a half-day's worth of pleasure.

At 2 P.M., we skittered off over a chop that unhinged the knees. We motored past the break in the rock wall of the Behm where the Chickamin River spills its green out onto the darker canal. The cloud ceiling started to lift and the sun occasionally poked a finger through the wet gray overhead.

### SIDE TRIP TO WALKER COVE

Six miles past the Chickamin, we turned into Walker, a real fjord, steeper, higher, narrower, and more beautiful than anything we had yet seen. The sun played fitfully on the blues and grays up and down the chasm walls and flashed in the 1,000-foot runs of snow melt that laced down through the greens of moss. Banks and I got out our cameras and made the most of the dramatic lighting. We cruised about, selecting angles and views, racing the fading light.

We had supper on the little river that comes into Walker. Seal were snorkeling in the river, looking for sockeye; the fish were flipping fin over tail at the river mouth. Back out on the Behm again, we ran toward a low-lying sun that blinked across a thousand small surfaces on the waves. Lower than the mountains, an Alaska rainbow made an arch of color, promising good weather for the morning.

We had had our respite and it was time to shove off for Petersburg, 130 miles north of Bell Island. Petersburg is the site of a salmon cannery; more importantly, it is the jumping-off point for the icefield of the LeConte Glacier, a side trip of high adventure on Alaskan waters. An early start is called for. There are no side trips on the way to Petersburg, but this is the stretch in which whale are most frequent; Clarence Strait is smack on their migration route.

In the early morning of our eighteenth day out, we took the Norseman out of the Behm Canal with Revillagigedo Island to port. Once into the Clarence we found the chop up to old tricks: shake, rattle and roll.

"Is this all the kind of water we are going to have in this cotton-pickin' Alaska?" muttered Portrey.

An hour out of Bell, Portrey spoke up again. "There they are," he said in a bellow. "There they are!"

I climbed on deck and started looking for porpoise off the bow, but Portrey was looking way up ahead; there, a mile in front of us, a plume about the size of a small tree was drifting slowly with the wind. Then another pushed up to join the first. We had run onto two whale, feeding, blowing, and cruising chummily side by side. We readied the cameras, and opened the Norseman up, chop be damned. Two blue-black lines in the water stayed in sight as we came toward them. There was no question: we'd run into a ménage of blue whales—phenomenal luck.

We eased the throttle and carefully drew closer, not wanting to disturb the man of the house. The huge backs slipped under just before we got there. We cut the engines entirely and waited.

One, two and three minutes passed. Then, "Bwaaaawhoosh!" Fifty yards astern, one of them surfaced with a noise like a punctured boiler. The spume was still hanging when he dropped under again. He resurfaced quickly, gave a heartfelt "Hasshhhh," emitted spume again and lay there, rolling slightly in the swell, visible at the blow holes and 25- or 30-feet behind that: a huge, ugly reef of flat slippery flesh, slightly awash.

The Norseman purred toward him slowly, cameras clicking. The back disappeared, a huge fin appeared, rolling into the air and then down again into the surface, followed by more back rolling into view; the horizontal tail, suspended from the huge trunk, moved slowly up out of the water, a 6- or 8-foot span from one tip to the other; it hung in the air, then lifted abruptly and went under.

"A 50-footer or better," breathed Portrey.

Both of them now surfaced, blew, and swam slowly south together, gigantic backs scarred, barnacled, gleaming wet, twice the size of the Norseman. We pressed them a bit, and they went under, lazily, each waving with the flip of the huge tail as a last gesture. We chased them for a half hour, trying to pick out the next surfacing area. (Dolly Connelly, hearing of the encounter some weeks later, wrote me that the pair we had observed were distracted by *l'amour*—you know about whales? asked Dolly—and therefore conveniently milled around for us instead of traveling their usual compass course to the South Pacific.)

The whales, nevertheless, did move slowly south. We puttered after them like a lovelorn interloper. As they got used to us, we maneuvered closer and closer without causing them to sound. At one point we nearly got too close. Banks, sitting on the forward hatch, held up a warning hand. We slowed down and watched, fascinated, as the tail came up and hung somewhere not quite directly over Banks' head, its breadth matching the beam of the boat. Then it moved into a downward

Thar she spouts!

Not one, but two blue whales.

We get closer and closer.

And closer: even the blowhole is
visible at these quarters.

90

Whale does a jackknife dive.

And waves good-bye. . . .

slide. ("Just before the tail came up," Banks said later, "I could look right down on that whale's tail under water. It was throbbing up and down, up and down.")

We turned north and ran for Petersburg with plenty to talk about all the way in.

At Petersburg, we berthed at wharves filled with fishing craft. There were so many they looked like a regatta of small and large tugs, lying to the club dock. Ashore, Portrey took us to meet a friend of his, Galen Biery, the foreman at the American Pacific Fisheries' cannery.

Biery took us to the canning shed and showed us through the assembly line. At the front end, shining salmon bodies are gutted automatically by a cutting machine that is known as the Iron Chink. Next, a revolving knife operation reduces the salmon to a pink meaty mash; this is tunneled off to a set of arm-length plungers that stuff the meat into tin cans; the cans are sealed by the next machine and steamed under pressure. The cooked-salmon tins are then dumped into a slide and packed into cartons by girls at the rate of 220 to 260 cans a minute, $\frac{1}{2}$-pound and 1-pound sizes, ready for your favorite supermarket.

Despite the presence of the cannery, Petersburg is not the place to get salmon cheap. Before the cans can be sold, they must be shipped to Bellingham or Seattle. Some are shipped back to Petersburg and are sold at a price 50 cents higher than in Seattle or San Francisco.

Petersburg is a good place for a haul-out if your yacht needs one. Four marine railways service the fishing fleet, and at least one of them is likely to be unoccupied at a given time.

We slept aboard that night, determined to start early for *the* high point of the trip: a visit to the LeConte ice field and an attempt to penetrate to LeConte Glacier itself.

# 9

## *The Glacier*

THE PENETRATION of the LeConte ice floe is strictly for skippers with cool heads and plenty of experience. Any competent yachtsman, however, can approach LeConte and see the ice at the entrance of the arm. The pack provides a spectacle you are not likely to match during the rest of the trip—or on any other trip, for that matter.

In the first few minutes of running toward the LeConte (12 miles off) the next morning, we discerned the nearest bergs, visible as a low, smudgy white apron against the shore far down the sound where the glacier enters Frederick Sound. LeConte is not a mild, easily visited, house-broken glacier, but a tidewater glacier guarded by an ice pack; it is on the move, crunching down from the mountains, forever dropping bergs into the LeConte Arm.

A glacier is basically an ancient collection of snow. It starts as a simple snow patch, but in a climate where the snow patch grows deeper by the century instead of clearing up in the spring, the snow becomes ice under the pressure of new snow above. The glacier moves to the sea from far mountains, forced on by the immeasurable bulk of snow and ice that builds up along its back, eon after eon. At first the snow becomes white ice, then, as it is buried deeper, blue ice; finally, at the bottom level, translucent black-green ice, hard as marble, cold as chilled steel.

At 10:30 we passed our first little chunk of ice, 3 feet across, rising half a hand out of the water; below the surface, it had size and weight enough to handily split our ship wide open, should we be so unlucky as to make hard contact.

Closer to the LeConte entrance we could see the larger bergs streaming along

Through large bergs and in toward the entrance of LeConte Arm.

the dark shores on either side of the entrance, a herd of white sheep jogging on their way among the currents.

We sped past the first large bergs at a distance of a hundred feet or so. They were not really high—5 or 6 feet average. (Mountain-size icebergs occur only off Greenland.) Below the surface, these LeConte bergs go down some 20 or 30 feet, giving them a heavy pendular motion in the water. They rose and fell ever so slightly in the wake of the boat as we headed for the entrance.

The bergs got bigger as we moved in. Some, as we approached, rose 20 feet, islands of ice sculpture, carved and shaped by sun and wind and the erosion of the water that would eventually absorb them.

The entrance to LeConte was marked by an exterior guard of bergs and low-lying pack ice. The royal blue water of the LeConte current, hung with this ice,

*94*

Inside LeConte: Portrey weaves the Norseman in and out of the pack ice.

was spreading into the gray of the Frederick. A stream of sea mist passed over the bergs, a cool aerial river. We glided into the edges of this new world: acres of ice, packed and pinnacled, pieces smaller than the boat, pieces bigger, all quietly rocking outside the entrance.

Portrey leaned over the wheel, looking for a passage to the entrance. He knelt on the helmsman's seat for a better view and finally found a small path between two fleets of pack ice. We edged carefully into the breach and proceeded into the pack; inside, it was more open; we reached a small lake within; we were still outside the LeConte entrance, but we cut our engines to hear the lap of waves smacking ice and the slap and drip of water falling off ice into ocean. The sun struck the bergs and set them afire with light—blue and white and green, opal and turquoise and crystal.

These are the big bergs, the kind that you go around for ten minutes.

We floated the dinghy so that Banks and I could photograph the hull against some of the dozen handsome tall bergs at the shallows of the entrance; these were 30-footers, apexed and turreted. Portrey volunteered to get us a picture that no one else, he assured us, would have. He said he would run the Norseman under a projecting arm of one of the bergs. He waved at a 6-foot arm of ice projecting from a monster berg. We pointed out that if the limb broke off while he was under it, he would have a bottomless yacht, but Portrey said that as long as he did not rock the berg before he got to it, the arm would hold.

Waiting until the water was quiet, Portrey moved the boat smoothly under the glittering projection on the blue monster. He slid the Norseman under and we triggered the cameras. He was out. I exhaled. Just to remind Portrey that it could happen, a low muffled roar came from elsewhere in the ice field, the noise that an arm makes when it lets go and slides down the parent berg into the ocean.

Banks and I boarded again and Portrey dodged into the narrow, shallow entrance itself, skirting giant bergs temporarily stranded by the outgoing tide. They tipped at crazy angles like foundered ships.

By 1:30 Portrey had us well into the interior of the LeConte, motoring along in floating ice of all kinds, big and small. Half a mile ahead was a flock of big bergs; beyond that, a huge tight sea of pack ice lay chunking together like chips in a cocktail shaker. The pack ice stretched as far as Thunder Point, and surely ran beyond it. All we knew was that we had to get around Thunder to have a look at the seldom-reached face of LeConte Glacier.

We motored slowly up to the ice pack, and Portrey, taking a critical look, said he thought we could work our way through. He picked his spot and put the nose of the Norseman against the apron of the pack. He slowly wedged two chunks apart with the bow. There was a horrid scraping sound as if from giant fingernails. Portrey ignored this and wedged two more chunks apart and then two more. He worked toward an open area just beyond the border of the pack, pivoting, spinning the boat like a top, squeezing through, spotting opportunities like a chess master. He found passage where I saw none. Banks and I assisted him by trying to move the pieces of pack ice away from the sides of the boat with pike poles. On my first try, I leaned over the side with the pole solidly against a 2-footer and shoved. It was like trying to move a reef. Each of the little chunks weighed thousands of pounds.

Portrey was heading for the left side of the arm. There, a line of blue water seemed to be opening up. We progressed to the screech and crackle of breaking ice and the thunderous scratching of submarine ridges. Portrey tailwagged through, wheedled, nosed chunks aside, skidded around boat-size bergs and avoided the occasional giant that reared grotesquely among the rest. We went round a bright blue berg and then a white one. Both resisted the boat effortlessly when we tried our puny power against their inertia.

The sky above alternately rained and cleared: cloud, sun, drip, overcast, and then sun again. A waterfall on shore alternately flashed and darkened like a white neon vein. The soft "srrr" of the engine could be heard only when the hull was not resonant with the crunching, scraping roar made by sharp edges as they moved past the underside. Portrey was literally shaving the ice to get us through.

At the rock wall of the arm, we found a little ribbon of a passage and the going became easier. We slugged our way slowly up to Thunder Point and around it. As we did so, the mist tore off the mountains that bedded the glacier and we saw the green-blue sheath of the LeConte, a mile off, crest after crest of ridged snow and ice descending from the mountains in rolling waves, shearing down to the sea in a green wall bristling with spines. Below it, the floe spread on the water like constellations of the starry night: nebulae of ice and blue supernova of bergs.

Portrey kept on. From 2 P.M. until 2:30, we made about 100 yards toward the glacier. Portrey said he thought the ice was getting thinner. The ice was not at all like lake ice; the dead unseen weight of it endowed our movements with a slow-motion unreality.

Near the glacier was a beautiful sharp pyramid of blue. We got to within three-quarters of a mile of the face, even with the great blue pyramid. It was hollowed on one side and convex on the other, a translucent shell. Portrey worked the boat out toward it. Banks and I got in the dinghy again and rowed away from the boat. From a distance, the Norseman was a piece of yellow flotsam in the jagged field of ice. Above the boat, the big berg, 30 feet high, rose like a cathedral transept, a huge shield, glowing in the sun's slant.

The water was calm. Each ice piece was a twin, reflecting itself in the absolute mirror of the green water. No ripples ran here. The only movement was in the ice undulating slowly on an unseen swell.

At 3:30, we were within half a mile of the face of the LeConte. Now there was no more room for us. We sat fast in the grip of the floe, engines off, just watch-

At the rock wall of the Arm, we found a little ribbon of a passage.

Beyond the pack ice, the great white wall of the glacier tumbles from the mountain.

ing. The face of the glacier tumbled down from the horizon, great shards of ice standing out on it, fathomless cleaved gaps running back into it. There was no sound but the hushed wearing of the ice. Seal lay on our right, in sanctuary, eyeing us warily. Behind us, the pack had closed, leaving not a trace of our path.

We drifted for at least five minutes, scanning the face of the glacier. Then we had a Scotch over glacial ice, formed several thousand years ago. I stuck one finger down into the water beside the boat and quickly pulled it back. The finger grew colder for the next twenty seconds. Survival time in these waters would certainly be a matter of only a few minutes.

All of us were alive to the possibility of tide and wind. If wind should rise and blow toward the glacier, we would be wedged in here behind a million tons of ice. The tide soon would be due to change and come in. This would have the

*100*

The strain of constant maneuvering and constant anxiety shows in Portrey's face.

Portrey collects ice for a Scotch on the rocks to celebrate—if we make it.

same effect. Under us, a current moved. The ice groaned ominously.

Portrey took his place at the helmsman's seat and put a hand reluctantly on the starter buttons. He kicked the engines over. The boat twisted, turned, spun in its own length and we started to work outward. We made our way slowly in the creak and moan of ice, none of us talking much. As we rounded Thunder Point, I looked back once more. The glacier had become an enormous green breaker, crashing down to the end of the arm, each fleck of foam hundreds of thousands of pounds of ice.

The wind did not rise; the ice did not close in. As we entered the welcome blue of the sea at the mouth of the LeConte, we ran the gauntlet of large bergs and left them behind in our wake, large agate gems of ice fire, a giant's treasure in the tide.

On the way out, the weirdly sculptured giants that we leave behind.

# 10

## *Terror, Taku, and Taku's Priest*

FROM Petersburg, Juneau is 120 miles off: a day's run could have ended the cruise now. But there are, in between, three side trips that in some ways surpass the previous ones. The first of these is the narrows of Fords Terror, the arm of arms along the Alaskan coast, a chasm of beautifully layered rock that leads to a calm, faraway tidal pool, under snow peaks. On our twentieth day we had just time to include Fords Terror in our itinerary—with a little pushing.

We curved out of Petersburg and headed for Endicott Arm, the reach that lies seaward of Fords. The weather was bad: fog. We had had seven days now of intermittent rain, drizzle, or fog, interspersed with sun. Today, on day seven of the fog-drizzle series, the sun was silver behind the bank of fog. We could see our breath on deck. I wore long underwear and was glad of it.

At 9:30 the fog thickened. Our worries increased. Not only was there a chance of running down another yacht, but in this stretch we could also run into a stray piece of ice off the LeConte Glacier. A small chunk could gut us the way the Iron Chink guts a salmon. I stood lookout while Banks computed the dead reckoning and Portrey steered and looked grim. We had been running longer by a considerable margin than Banks had calculated: still no shore ahead. And then, when land did come up faintly through the fog, it was running east rather than northwest. We had been set by the tide more than Banks had allowed for. We had run 3 or 4 miles into an arm south of our landfall on the mainland. Portrey turned and took us out along the shore, a dim ghost forest flickering in and out of sight. At 11:00 we were out into blue sky. There seemed to be a chop stirring out ahead of us. "No more chop, please," said Banks. We got one anyway.



The entrance to Fords Terror →

After two hours of counter-chop maneuvers by the three of us in the cockpit, we spotted the opening of the Endicott. We went in and left the chop behind, praise be. Top speed. In front of us and above were the twisted corrugations of a glacier mantling a high ridge. The glacier ran back into the mountains miles from the sea arm that it once covered and carved.

Endicott was a lake of still water that gave a green hue to the reflected towers of cloud; the cumulus was rising like volcanic steam over the filigree of snow on the mountains to the east. We chased a couple of young geese over the water. They paddled foot and wing, fanning out of the way like frenzied clockwork toys. We went past a couple of house-sized bergs, pale blue, with a surface texture like banana cream fill. A line of clouds lowered itself over the peaks rimming the western shore, but without cutting the sun off. The clouds lay contour on contour, threatening to roll down into the arm, but not quite doing so.

At 1:30, we turned into Fords Terror, slipped past a raft of small blue ice chunks, cornered a bend and pointed down a deep canyon, its sides striped with horizontal strata lines of gray, green, and ash-white.

The "terror" of Fords Terror lies in the strong tide action at the narrow throat we were approaching. The current in the throat is like a raging spring flood river most of the day, roaring into the arm or out of it. A yachtsman should never go in or out of Fords with the tide at his stern. The best plan is to go in at high slack tide and come back in about four hours, before the incoming tide gets going. If you overstay, you have to contend with the rip coming back. And it is truly a terror.

"What tide are we on?" I asked Portrey. "The wrong one," said Portrey. He meant we had missed high slack and were on the first of the outgoing tide which gave us a shorter time in which to make the end of the arm and get back.

We gunned up the still-not-strong current at the throat of Fords and into the main body of the arm. It was a gorgeous body. Green, soft-contoured mountain meadows run back from the very rim of the walls toward snow peaks. Riverlets pour from the meadows over the edge and down the walls, over rock faces, crashing from face to face in 100-foot streamers, washing rumpled squares of rock before falling into the water of the arm at the bottom.

Deeper into the arm, a white stream meandered down a long curving alpine meadow high over the boat. The cliffs were gray and glossy black, like ceramic tile walls. Ahead was a narrow cleft, 1,000 feet at each shoulder, framing a moun-

The pool at Fords Terror: a ring of green surrounded by snow peaks and mountain meadows.

tain dead on the bow. We moved through the cleft into the loveliest spot in Alaska, if one has to be picked: a pool of green in a bowl of mountain with forests and streams running down the far side. The sides, striated with traces of rose-colored rock, are draped with white filaments of water that come from the folds of a soft green valley above. Alternate gray and rose of rock, green of growth and white of melting snow, layer after layer, ascended to a peak brushed by clouds.

We let the boat drift in the pool and had lunch to the rustle of water down the cliff sides. We felt the cool rush of wind from the peaks and breathed the fragrance of fir from the shore; we watched the play of light and shadow along the ebony ledges.

We limited our time and, at that, we overstayed. Portrey put on all steam after lunch. We went bee-lining back out the series of chasms, setting off flocks of white tern that wheeled and lifted gracefully. We sailed into the now-oncoming tide at the throat. The tidal water was at full flood, ripping, bounding, forming maelstrom and counter-maelstrom; foaming crests threw themselves at one another.

Portrey moved the boat carefully into the charging currents. He gunned cannily from backwater to backwater, powering upward in spurts, sometimes making no more than a few feet at a time; at last, in a final zigzag, he flipped us up over the top of the fall and we leveled off, leaving the white curling waters unmarked by our passage.

After Fords Terror, there are two other side trips that break up the run to Juneau. First is Taku Harbor, a delightful anchorage. The second, somewhat farther north, is Taku River Lodge, set across the Taku River from Hole-In-the-Wall glacier: the lodge runs a daily boat to the lake formed by the Twin Glaciers.

We decided to pass up Taku Harbor for the moment. We headed for the glacier country of the Taku River. To reach the Taku River Lodge before dark, Portrey drove the Norseman mercilessly. Stephens Passage seemed a long, long run. We turned toward land where the Taku River came broad and green out of the mountains, flowing from Canada across the Alaskan panhandle into the sea. As we moved in, we saw Canadian mountains rising behind Alaskan mountains, two chains forming a jagged shambles, broken pie crust dusted with cane sugar.

Once in the river, we were in half-light. But we could see a long finger of snow thrust out from a side valley to the edge of the river: the Taku Glacier. We came even with it; the glacier was a furrowed flow inundating the ridges that bore it, a flow channeled and rippled and edged in gold by the sun; and as the sun settled further the face of the glacier became a high shadowy wall over a gleaming strip of shore.

Portrey and Banks were not watching the glacier. They were scanning the milky brown of the river, a silt curtain hiding everything under the surface. "Hope we get by the mud," said Portrey, staring straight ahead. "Might as well go fast as slow, though." Portrey's idea was that by going fast he would give the hull a chance to skip over any mud we happened to strike. The Norseman skimmed across the surface, none of us knowing whether 40 feet or 4 inches lay under the bow.

"Stop!" shouted Banks. "Stop her!" We did stop, with a bash and then a scraping crunch. There we sat, high on the slick and gleaming top of a mudbank. The silty brown water streamed from under the hull in little rivers that ran over the mud into the tide; the tide was fast ebbing, and the boat getting drier by the minute.

We decided to anchor her and make the lodge by dinghy—there was no attraction in a night on the bank. The three of us squeezed down into the dinghy, pushing off with oars and a mop handle through the mud until she floated clear. It was only a mile upstream to the lodge dock.

Taku Lodge is a small tourist establishment with a main lounge and dining room plus small bedroom cabins. Most guests fly down from Juneau. We were the second hull to try the river that season. Our main interest was to take the river trip up to the Twin Glaciers on a tributary stream of the Taku. The trip ($7.50 a head) is run on a river boat captained by a lodge employee who knows where all the mudbanks are. We signed on for the morning trip.

After dinner, I stood out on the lawn under the night sky and watched the moonlight come over a tongue of Hole-In-the-Wall Glacier across the river. It was a beautiful but uncanny sight in the lunar radiance, curling down from a visible peak and spreading over an entire mountain before dropping into the river like a great flow of white lava.

The following morning we loaded into the flat-bottom river boat with the crew. The captain, a young college student working at Taku, sent her flying up over

The slowly flowing river of ice: one of the Twin Glaciers.

the silty river. A mile up, following the sufficient but invisible channel through mud flats, we ran past an eagle's nest beside the river; the parent flapped about in menacing circles and junior stuck a beaky brown head over the edge of the jumble of sticks at the 60-foot level of the fir.

We turned into a tributary, whizzing past chunks of clear ice coming downstream, and then into a small rapid, boiling brown with mud. The 35-hp outboards on the stern screamed as they strained up the rapid. At the top we entered the sudden stillness of a lake and here were the Twin Glaciers—two landslides of riven ice coming down to the lake's edge at the far side. There were white bergs bobbling about in the darker water: ice cream in a ginger ale float.

This is a rare bird among glacial sites: hot springs at the edges of the lake push its temperature above the freezing point; the lake is a mix of melted glacier and spring water. Instead of traveling downstream, the bergs melt off here in the lake, forming the major source for the water of the tributary. So formidable is the melting process that there is no real ice pack as there is at LeConte. We could go as near to the faces as we cared to. We already could see the interior of the deep blue glacial chasms of the face, shaping bergs that would drop off into the water. On top, the glaciers were a twisted map of ridges and piled ice.

About three hundred yards off one glacier, we could hear the crackling of the ice as it fissured under the impact of our wake. We made several passes, hoping to startle a berg into birth. Suddenly there was a sound like a landslide and a roll of thunder. Part of the glacier face cracked loose, descended with deliberate speed into the water, sank almost under and then rose to a peak, and settled back, bobbing ponderously, a brand-new berg, about two boats long and one boat high.

After lunch the captain and his crew, to prove to us that it could be done, took us off to the hot-spring edges of the lake where they water-skied behind the river boat. One fall into this water and a boy is pretty much through for the day by the time he turns pink again.

We returned to the lodge. Then we were taken downstream to the Norseman. She was pulling against her anchors like a stallion on a halter. We were anxious to stop at Taku Harbor before we made our final northward landfall that night. Father Hubbard, the famous Jesuit geologist, explorer, and Alaskan authority, made Taku Harbor his home at that time. (He has since died.)

We took it easy going downriver, staying in the channel. Mark Twain in his

112

Closing in on the foot of the glacier, Portrey and I hope we'll see an iceberg born.

The foot of the glacier riven with chasms.

best river-boat days would have found the Taku respectably tough. The river bed is shiftier than the Mississippi's. This time we made it without loss of bottom paint.

We came into Taku Harbor in the afternoon and found Father Hubbard sitting on the front porch of the bunkhouse. The scholarly Jesuit we met was a small man, an old man, but with something of his former wiry frame still suggested. One arm hung across his belt, almost useless from a stroke; a pair of jet-black eyebrows sat at a quizzical forty-five-degree slant over eyes that were dark and big. Those eyes had looked closer at Alaska than any others during the thirty-three years of his explorations.

The sun was moving across Taku Harbor, throwing the old cannery dock into relief and whitening a moon above. Father Hubbard told us of salmon runs of the old days where the fish packed so close that the rustle of dorsal fins through the water made a distinct noise, like a hundred brooms dragged across the floor. He spoke of friends who came to visit him here, to stay with him, sometimes for whole summers. "They just come here for the peace and no telephones and no tension."

*114*

The top, twisted by wind and stress.

One of his old friends was on hand, Tiger Olsen, a Swede in his eighties, a great shouter—when Tiger talks, he shouts. He liberally interrupted Father Hubbard and swore blue without hesitation. "One of the few old-timers left," said the priest, "and utterly honest." Tiger had homesteaded ("patented") in Taku for forty or fifty years, raising potatoes and canning deer, sometimes making a few assays for mining companies.

Father Hubbard told us that his usual considerable income from his film work had been jeopardized. Taku had just had six weeks of rain and fog. Father Hubbard reported that he and Olsen and the two young photographers and the housekeeper had all been snarling at each other for days.

"Well, like it or not, it's the rain that makes this land what it is," said Father Hubbard. "There's no topsoil here so the trees all pancake on the rock and it rains so much they make their own humus."

Father Hubbard told us that Hole-In-the-Wall and its twin, Taku Glacier, have been advancing mightily in the past few years, both reaching down to the river. All the other arms of the Juneau ice cap have been receding. Father Hubbard said

The hot waters of the glacial lake shape the bergs into free forms.

that he thought it was because more snow had collected on the Taku side; the ice cap had "tilted" and the ice was now running downhill toward the Taku and pulling back along the other edge to the north.

The talk ran from the mysterious ice islands of the Arctic (the Arctic has no icebergs—the ice there is seldom more than 6 feet thick) to the economy of Alaska. "This state has tremendous potential," said Father Hubbard. "What it needs is a stable population. Half the people up here are in Army or Government jobs. There are people coming to Alaska, yes, but just as many are going."

Father Hubbard distinguished between "Alaskans" who want to die here, and those others who come up to take what they can and leave. "In the last elections," said Father Hubbard, "the 'other people' voted the resident Alaskans out of everything they wanted.

Resting after lunch on the lake of the Twin Glaciers.

"If this land had been in Europe, a dozen wars would have been fought over it. It has every metal and the only decent tin deposit in the country."

As he talked about the new state, the moon over it lighted up steadily. When the moon was fully gold, we got up and thanked the old priest for his hospitality. "Come back" he said. "You probably will. Look at me, busted up as I am. I'm back."

We headed for Juneau in the night. The mountains rose dark and protective overhead. The moon lit our way over the water. Before midnight, we turned off the moonstruck channel and came into the harbor at Juneau to finish our twenty-first and last day on the road north. We had come well over 1,000 miles, had had one minor repair on the stove, no holes in the hull. Our worst problem had been a small leak, which had sprung somewhere in the stern. We would have that fixed in the morning.

We made for the Baranof Hotel, a first-class establishment, and we showered, shaved, and got used to the feel of a suit coat. For our first big meal, we went to Laura Lee's Bar B Q, where the spiced beef was fit celebration for the completion of our long bout of seamanship.

Any competent skipper could have made the cruise north, but only Portrey and Banks, I felt, could have made it with all the side trips and all the fishing in the relatively short time given us. That night we had the pleasant feeling that we had all taken part in something unique.

Juneau is civilization as city people know it. The Baranof was exemplary and we made the most of it. There was a *choice* of good restaurants in town. Mike's and the Douglaston Club were two. We ate our way through the best we could buy while we concluded our business. Mine was to get air passage for the trip back and write the story; Portrey and Banks supervised the fixing of the hull preparatory to their taking the Norseman back to Bellingham. The yard found a slight separation at the transom at one point.

Portrey and Banks were in a hurry. They had only six days left of their four-week vacation, and they were going to make it back in six, too.

On our second evening in Juneau we did a little more celebrating, this time of my status as a sourdough. There are various methods prescribed for becoming a sourdough, none of them really fit to print, all involving either bears, Eskimo women, or the Yukon River. We were content with our own definition: "Get here in your own boat from the mainland states—all in one piece."

The next afternoon I flew back to Seattle, sitting comfortably on a Northwest Orient airliner, looking down at a hundred yet unexplored passages and a thousand islands in the great water road rippling and glowing below: the Inside Passage.

# 11

## *Back Down*

PORTREY and Banks made it back to Campbell River in six days despite terrible weather. They left Juneau at 12 noon and saw two whales outside, but did not stop to chase them. They arrived at Petersburg at 5:30 and, in the rain, tried to make Ketchikan that night. ("It rained all the way down," Portrey told me later, "you missed the best part of the trip.") They didn't make Ketchikan: north of the town of Wrangel, one of the pistons on one engine went out. Portrey found that they could still hold their speed pretty well, so they anchored in a bay for the night and decided not to stop for repair.

On the second day of their return trip the two men ran into heavy weather out of Meyers Chuck in Clarence Strait. Gale warnings were out and the wind was blowing at 45 mph. They tried to buck it and made 9 miles in the next three hours. They found a small jut of land to anchor behind, finally, and laid low to wait for the storm to blow itself out. They had to stand watch and keep the anchor in place. If the anchor had dragged, it would have dropped into deep water and the boat would have then been out in the storm again.

At 8 A.M. on the third day Portrey and Banks were able to continue to Ketchikan. They had breakfast there, gassed and went on to Prince Rupert, arriving at 4 P.M. They went on again after dinner and got to Butedale at 10:30 on a pitch-dark night.

The next day the Norseman crossed Milbanke Sound and arrived at Bella Bella at noon; the two ate lunch and were off for Alert Bay. They hit extremely rough water near Namu, however, and were forced to stop there overnight. Gale warnings were out again.

They started off at 4 A.M. the next morning and made it out onto Queen Charlotte Sound. Portrey said, "We should not have tried it." It took them twelve hours to cross the 65 miles to Alert Bay. "The waves," Portrey wrote, "got so steep we could stand up and drink from them." Both the men and the boat took a terrible beating. They got to Alert at 4 P.M.

On the sixth day the Norseman left Alert Bay at 5 A.M. and got to Campbell River at 9:30 P.M. Portrey and Banks slept in a hotel. "Did that hot bath and those clean sheets feel good!" Portrey said later.

The Norseman departed Campbell River at 8 A.M. the following morning and reached Bellingham at 5:30 P.M. They had a late dinner, and Portrey said, "I felt we deserved a last meal on *Sports Illustrated*."

That's not quite all. The rugged trip down, coupled with the vibration set up by the missing piston, finally worked the hull so much that it opened up at the transom again. When Portrey came down to the dock in the morning, Norseman, Mercury engines and all, was on the bottom.

"Now that made for a striking situation," said Portrey.

The boat was duly raised and engines disassembled and dried out to save them from corrosion. I told Portrey that it served as a warning to those who drive boats too hard. But Portrey concluded, "It was a swell trip and actually nothing happened that I didn't anticipate other than the boat sinking and, actually, that was minor."

# *Practical Matters*

## 1. GAS AND MILEAGE

Seattle to Juneau with side trips: 1,365 miles
Return trip: 880 miles

Gas mileage: 1½ miles per gallon
Cost of gas and oil: $681
Cost per mile of gas and oil: $.26

## 2. GEAR AND SUCH

*Comfort:* If I were to do the trip all over again, I would install spring-loaded chairs capable of handling the bounce of the hull without dislocating the vertebrae of the sitter. These chairs would be worth whatever they cost.

*Safety:* I arrived in Seattle with the firm intention of getting an inflatable life raft aboard. This was my number-one safety point. The only one I could find in Seattle, however, was big enough to take up the whole cockpit even in deflated form. Portrey demurred. He felt the dinghy would do it. I still feel that the average yachtsman, which Portrey certainly is not, should have a raft. It should be inflated and tied topside when an open stretch is coming up.

*Engine:* You should either have twin engines or travel with another yacht. In a tide run or a strong wind you have to have a second engine available in case your first engine quits. The rock-wall nature of the shore demands it.

*Life jackets:* A foam cushion does not constitute a life jacket in these waters. You must have a vest type that can be tied firmly to your person.

*Navigation aids:* The course is fully buoyed, thanks to the United States and Canadian Governments, who look out for the fishing fleets. There is a good system of navigation lights for night running as well.

*Windshield wiper:* Portrey insisted on electric windshield wipers plus the wash-pump installation, and so would I if I were going again. You must have these to maintain speed in sea spray.

*Flare:* Carry a signal flare gun and dry flares.

*Radio:* You must carry a receiving set that has been adjusted to the British Columbia and Alaska weather bands. A Seattle marine outfitter can do it. On the sending side, you should have, at a minimum, one of the Gibson Girl type automatic SOS senders with balloon aerial. If you should be stranded, this might be the difference between adventure and tragedy.

*Charts:* Get the Northwest Marine Atlas Volumes I and II. These are perfect cruising charts, section by detailed section. You need a couple of over-all strategy maps from the Hydrographic Office and the United States Coast and Geodetic Survey series and that is all. Bryant's in Seattle has the atlases and the maps. Of course, these charts are no good unless you have swung your ship so that you know exactly what your compass deviations are.

*Fuel:* The fishing depots take care of this; the distance between them can be up to 100 miles, however, so your fuel capacity should be sufficient for at least that distance. The corollary is that you should know to the tenth how much fuel your engines burn at one-quarter, half, three-quarters and full throttle. Otherwise you have no data on which to make decisions. At least a few of these decisions will be fairly crucial; you can count on that.

*Repairs:* Avoid fishing-depot mechanics whenever possible. Wait for a marine railway or at least an honest-to-God marine mechanic. He can be found at the principal towns along the routes: Nanaimo, Pender Harbor, Campbell River, Alert Bay, Prince Rupert, Ketchikan, Petersburg, and Juneau. Any big salmon cannery will have mechanics trained to repair fishing boats, and such mechanics are often expert at outboard and inboard repair.

*Spark plugs:* These deserve special mention in outboard cruising. Check them once a

day, and remove any that show signs of fouling. Replace them all at least once a week. You should have a kit of spare parts for all vulnerable gear. Otherwise, you may need to have replacements flown in to you along the route.

*Clothes:* Temperatures run from the mild eighties to the frosty forties. You will need long underwear, two sets. Also two pairs of wool pants, two heavy sweaters, and a complete set of rubberized foul-weather gear. (If you have the old stiff rain gear, invest in a new pliable foul-weather outfit.) I suggest that you take a good warm ski or hunting parka with insulated interlining.

Your summer wear is pretty standard. I found that I wore shorts and short-sleeved shirts less than half the time, so there is no need to stock more than two each of these.

*Shoes:* A pair of good heavy hiking boots of waterproof leather is the answer to long days of standing in the cockpit with the chop bouncing away at the hull. It really isn't too comfortable to sit in this situation, so it can mean three or four hours of standing per day. You need the boots for shore walks anyway.

Slitted deck sneakers (Topsiders) are fine for anything else—fishing, coming into harbor, and so on, whenever you need to leave the cockpit.

*Headgear:* The long-billed cap is an investment in comfort for the eyes. You should also have a regular sou'wester for rain. During the trip, I lost my sou'wester and made do with an impregnated-fiber hat of fire engine red which my cruise companions sometimes persuaded me to wear ashore. They said that it was a proper Northwest visiting hat.

124

*Sunglasses:* Get a good pair, made from optical-grade glass. If you wear prescription glasses, have your sunglasses made to the prescription. Get them as dark as possible. Optical-grade glass is imperative since it is the only glass that really screens out ultraviolet, the harmful component of the sun's rays. Otherwise you are just darkening your vision, causing the eyes to open and receive more, rather than less, harmful ultraviolet. Even if you do not normally wear sunglasses, wear them this trip. There is a lot of difference between standing the sun for a set of tennis and having to stare out over bright, backlit wave patterns for hours on end.

*Insect repellent:* Take two or three spray cans along.

*Heater:* A good kerosene heater can be useful to dry wet clothes and to take the edge off a chill evening. (The heater should not be run at night, for safety reasons.)

## 3. THE HULL

There are two ways to take the Inside Passage, as I have said.

The fast and furious method requires a relatively light outboard hull with twin 25-hp engines or better. Or it requires an inboard planing hull with at least twice that amount of power. Outboard and inboard planing hulls of this sort can make 20 to 35 mph. This means you can often bite off 60 to 140 miles in the morning and still have the afternoon to fish, explore, or relax. The planing hull can buck any tide along the coast, including some 15-knot rips that stand in the way. This hull can handle weather, it can run from it, or it can wait for a better break. It offers the delicious privilege of giving in to impulse without necessarily getting behind schedule.

On the adverse side, the planing hull is not terribly comfortable, and it can become terribly uncomfortable. Once you have invested in this much horsepower, you are committed to using it. You also have to watch ceaselessly for flotsam, since it can seriously damage the hull at high speed.

And the navigation problems demand that you stay awake on pain of missing a turn and having to backtrack. The hull is built for speed and handling, not for accommodations. The appointments tend to be Spartan, especially in the outboard.

In spite of some rugged days on the jarring deck, I admit to a sneaky liking for this kind of travel. Given the desire to go all the way to Juneau and back in four weeks, given scenery that is scaled to the gods and the will to make as many side trips into this scenery as possible, fast traveling and a certain callousness toward comfort is the only answer.

Equally surely, slow and steady cruising has arguments on its side. The nonplaning or displacement hull is built to breast the waves in serene succession without the slap and shake of the planing hull. It has a top speed of 6 to 16 knots, depending on power. Thus, the navigation problem is not as critical: there is more time to spot the turns. And, with a heavier hull plus lower speed, spotting surface obstacles becomes desirable

*125*

rather than essential. Also, the nonplaning hull can afford luxury accommodations, since weight-paring is not a prime requisite of design.

On the other hand, the slower hull has to take the weather as it comes. It can neither afford to wait nor does it usually have the option of running away. The slow hull has to figure on hitting the tide rips at the right hour. It has to count on using most of the daylight to make the hop from anchorage to anchorage. The displacement boat skipper is likely to be a deliberate fellow, used to planning and taking the long view. There is not much margin for impulse.

The slow and easy hulls are generally one of four types on Inside Passage waters.

The first type is the vintage hull, the favorite of the Canadian cruising man. No boat ever really retires along this coast. These are the long hulls with a wheelhouse forward, then a main salon, a kitchen (it would be misleading to call it a galley), bedrooms, and spacious fantail—all unaltered from the time of launching back in the 1930's or 1940's, a time when anyone who could afford a yacht was not one who would have any worries about how long it took him to get to Juneau.

Second, there are the modern displacement boats, the heavy motor yacht familiar to all yachtsmen.

Third, there are the work boats that have been converted. The work boat makes a nice roomy cruise boat and occasionally you see one. A recent meritorious design in a work boat by Jack Gooldrup of Gibsons Landing (north of Vancouver) was the fastest fishing boat on the coast. In 1961, when a sockeye school was sighted off Juan de Fuca unexpectedly, Bert Gooldrup, in one of his brother's designs, was the only upcoast gill netter who could get there fast enough to reach the school. The Gooldrup 33 will do 16 knots with a 150-hp engine and that is a good 3 or 4 knots above the usual for any but all-out planing hulls. This is a kind of compromise hull that makes real sense in the waters of the Inside Passage.

The fourth category of slow hulls is the sailing auxiliary. Unfortunately, sail is mostly wasted up here, except on open water. The wind tends to be violent and jumpy; in the passages it blows from dead ahead or dead astern. Beating up a narrows is too much to ask of a crew when the narrows are only a mile or so wide and 60 miles long. Running before the wind is possible, but can be a bit harrowing, due to the tendency of the wind to shift rapidly, calling for a corresponding jibe of the sails.

If, however, you can patiently plan for tides and distance on a 6- or 7-knot basis (average speed for a medium size auxiliary under power) then there is not a more comfortable, sea-kindly vessel to be had for this trip than an auxiliary.

Be a speedster and bear it, or be a leisurely sailor and arrive later. Whichever you choose, the rewards will more than make up for either the time or the discomfort involved. If beauty anywhere in the world can take your mind off small dissatisfactions, and make big ones seem small, then you will find that beauty along the Inside Passage.

## 4. THE TIME FACTOR

Besides the limit placed on you by the hull, there is the limit of total vacation time.

The fast-hull plan of the cruise can take you all the way to Juneau in a two-week vacation with a bare minimum of side trips.

If you take all the side trips, you can still make Juneau in a three-week vacation, given good weather.

Both the above plans anticipate storing the hull in Juneau at the end of the voyage, and doing the Inside Passage in reverse the following summer.

The more usual procedure is to take one week for the return trip. The entire return can be made in seven days if the weather is not unusually foul, but you have to be young in heart.

Another alternative is to stop short of Juneau. The essence of cruising is to have at least a third of the time set aside to do nothing but fish, sun or sight-see. A run to Alaska for the sake of covering distance is hardly a cruise in the best sense of the word.

The skipper with shorter time at his command can stay south of Queen Charlotte Sound and still have a crack at some of the most fascinating cruising on the continent.

## 5. SEASON AND TRAFFIC

June is generally best avoided, being a rain month. Beyond that, there is still an element of chance, but your best bet for sunny days is in July and August. The temperature is at peak then, and, starting July 15, the salmon begin to spawn along the coast; a spawning run is one of the most dependable excitements of the cruise.

There are few days when you won't see another hull. There are Inside Passage enthusiasts with home ports all along the coast of the state of Washington. The rest of the West's yachtsmen arrive overland, up from San Francisco, from Los Angeles, from as far away as Tucson and Amarillo, trailering their light outboard cruising rigs behind them. They launch in Puget Sound and you will find them all along the route as you proceed northward.

You will meet many more in the first section than in the last two, however. Customs officials report at least 2,000 yachts in the San Juan-Georgia Straits region every summer. About 500 yachts jump across Queen Charlotte to the next section, and another 250 yachts make it all the way across Dixon Entrance into Alaska, the greatest cruising ground of all.

## PHOTO CREDITS

Photographs on the following pages were taken by Clyde
Banks: 10, 17, 19, 34, 43, 50 (lower), 51, 62, 63, 66–67, 73,
76, 77, 81, 90 (lower), 91, 101, 102, 103, 105, 107, 113, 116,
117, 121, 122.


All other photographs by Morten Lund.